AF225718

Where's God?
Revelations Today
Photobook Companion:
GOD Signs
2nd Edition
BRYAN FOSTER
Book 4 in the 'GOD Today' Series

Published in 2018

Great Developments Publishers

Gold Coast, Queensland, Australia 4217

ABN: 13133435168 USA-EIN: 98-0689457

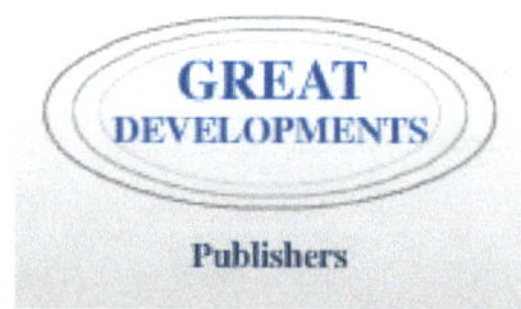

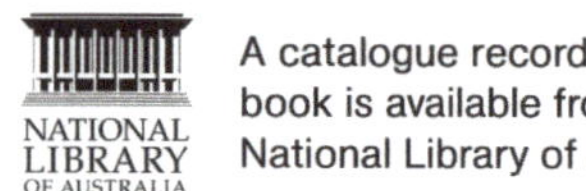

A catalogue record for this book is available from the National Library of Australia

ISBN: 978-0-6484001-8-9 (hardcover)

Creator: Foster, Bryan, 1957- author, photographer

Website: https://www.godtodayseries.com/where-s-god

Images: Bryan Foster - Copyright © Great Developments Publishers, 2018. Andrew Foster (Austographer.com) contributed.

Cover image: Easter Sun-Cross, Texas NSW/Qld Border, Australia

Back Cover Sun Images: Cylinder Beach, North Stradbroke Island + Mt Warning, Australia

Graphics: Bryan Foster and Bookpod

CONTENTS

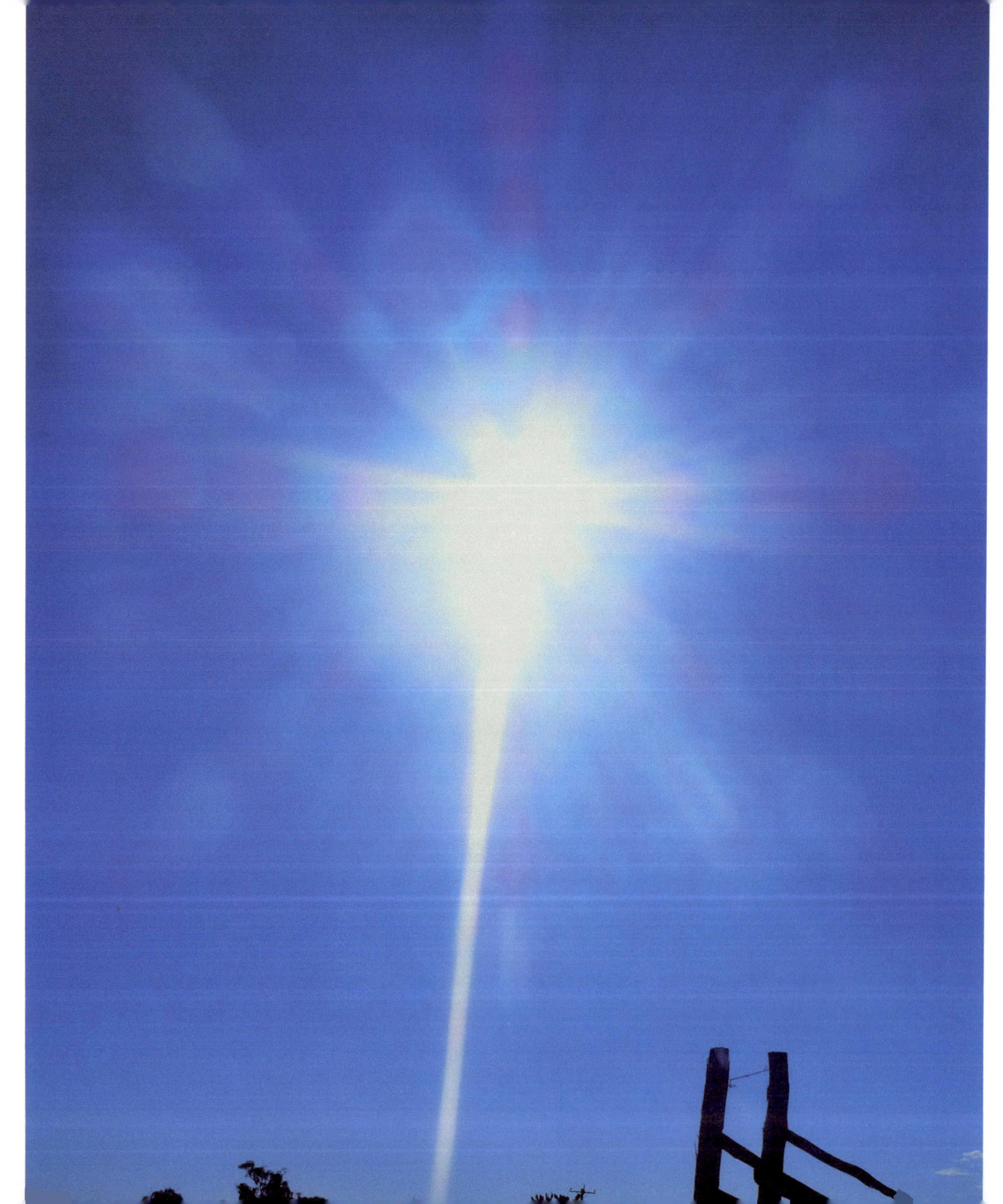

Introduction

Where's God? Revelations Today Photobook Companion: GOD Signs (2nd ed)

I now fully accept that the images and symbols contained in this photobook are all signs from God, encouraging and supporting us into sharing God's Revelations, inspired messages and experiences sent by God.

Hopefully, these stories and images will help you on your journey to God, seeking the Truth and needing God in your life, right up to the ultimate salvation with God after your life here on Earth.

The images you are about to view have challenged both my wife, Karen, and myself. You don't expect to see these types of photos just appear, and on numerous occasions.

Let's explore what we do know. The images had sun rays or arrows resulting from the sun and recorded photographically. These appear to be reflected or refracted sunlight on the lens. Could or would God use this means to make a point?

The big question I asked many times, "Why couldn't these signs come from God? After all, God does work through people and the things of this world." These images began almost two years after the Mt Warning Revelations were received. I was also continually reminded not to put God to the test.

Considering all the God experiences I have had for quite a while now, including the regular Tears from God, combined with the two direct Revelations received, one on my 25th birthday, the other two years ago on the plains of Mt Warning, plus my heavy involvement with God through the teaching of religious vocation and Church parish and deanery roles, actually makes so much sense of these latest photographic events.

Too many people doubt so much to do with God and religious institutions. In fact, the numbers of nonbelievers are ever increasing in the western civilisation. It is time to challenge humanity - again! Who says? God says!!!

This photobook's images won't please everybody. I anticipate some backlash. I can see many people asking the question, "Who does he think he is?" Others will yell, "It was the camera stupid!" While others will quietly reflect on the reality and see the authentic interpretation taken as a gift from God.

Many of the stories, inspired messages and Revelations found in both these books, *Where's God? Revelations Today* and this companion photobook, come with a physical aspect. Not just a spiritual belief but an actual physical dimension.

Such examples include the physical flow of heat passing from the charismatic religious sister's healing hands which were placed on my head, along with the subsequent flow of the Tears from God, on my 25th birthday.

These started these regular occurrences which have occurred over the decades since.

The next critical physical example once again ended with the gift of tears - the Tears from God.

These confirmed the Truth of the Revelations from God which were received on the plains of Mt Warning during a cold winter's night two years ago.

While recently this year the physical experiences of the sun rays, sun crosses, sun flares, sun arrows and double rainbows shared in this photobook, once again highlight God's heavy involvement.

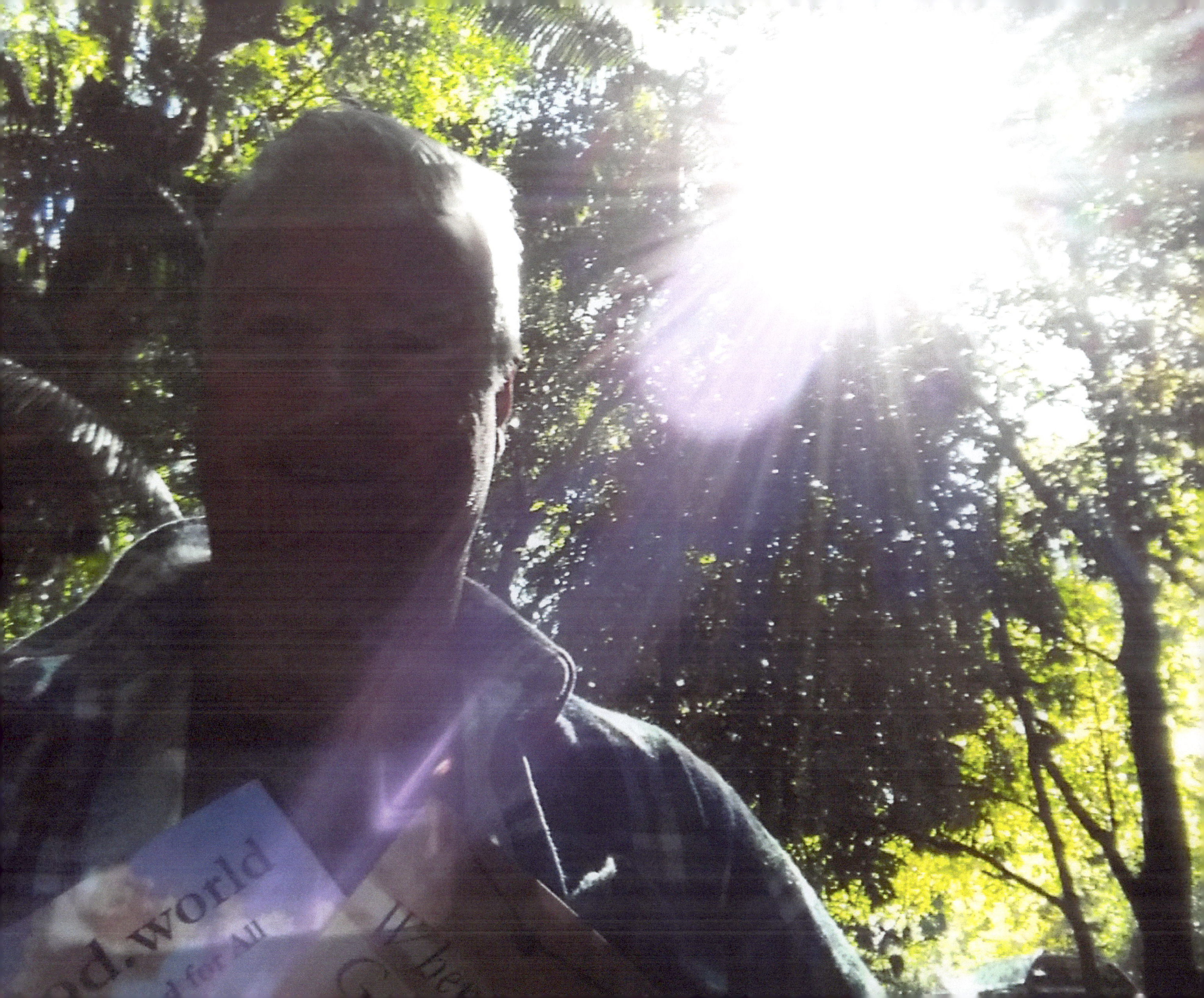
od.world
d for All
W

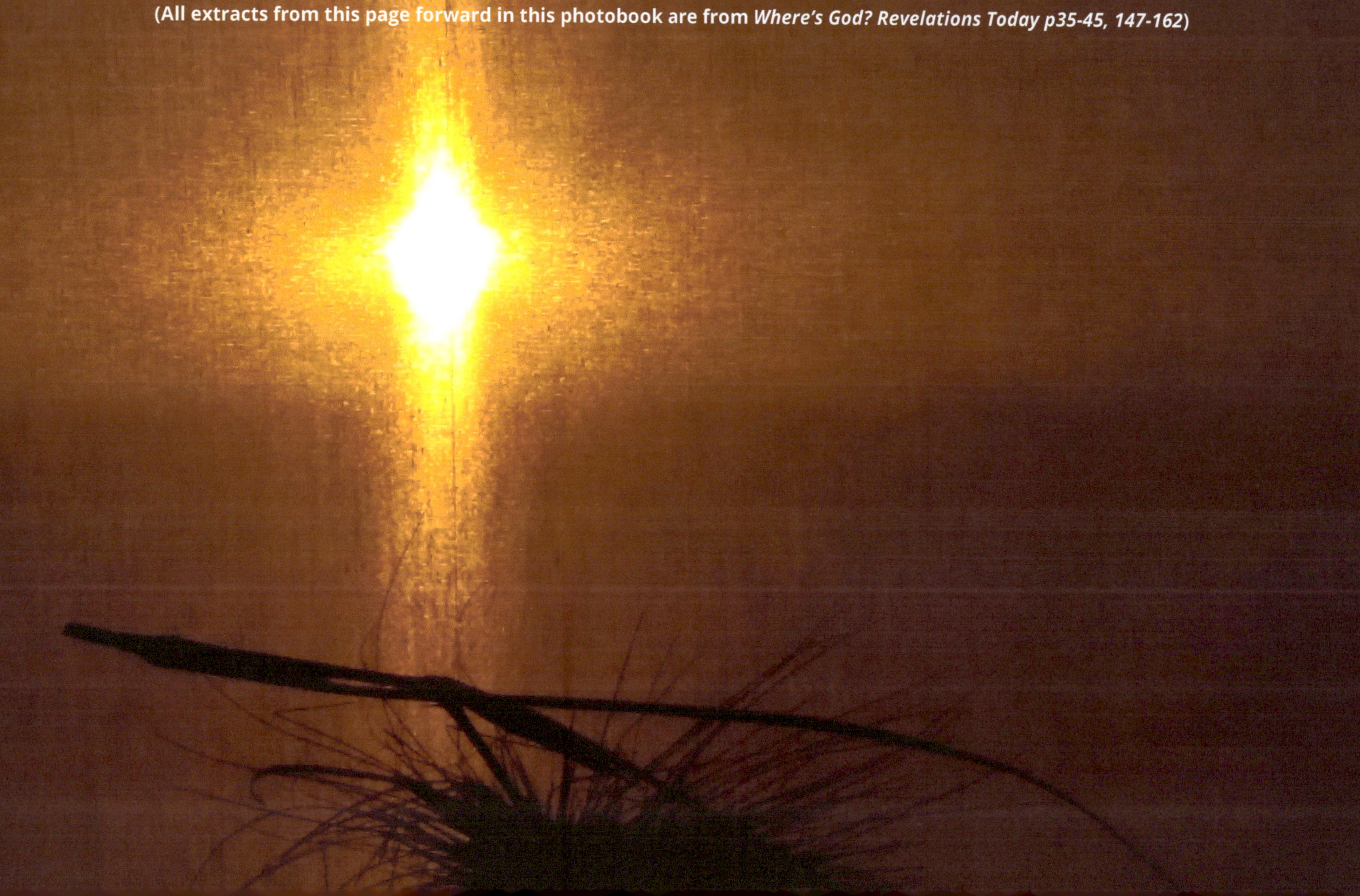

This photobook surprises the reader with some exceptional and different photographic images formed from various reflections and refractions of the sun. Some formed across the author, others with spectacular sun shapes formed in the sky.

These occurred at various venues, especially at the foot of Mt Warning, on Straddie, North Stradbroke Island and inland at Texas on the Queensland / New South Wales border.

The sun is seen as central for many people in their imagining of God and God's beyond-our-reality's awesome powers.

(All extracts from this page forward in this photobook are from *Where's God? Revelations Today p35-45, 147-162*)

Forward

Bryan has been in close contact with God for many years. I have been fortunate to have witnessed this first hand. *Where's God? Revelations Today* shares vital Revelations, inspired messages and stories. You are invited to explore some fascinatingly affirming messages from God for today's world.

This fourth book in his 'GOD Today' Series continues the journey of discovering God that began with *1God.world: One God for All*.   Bryan renews and continues the exploration of who God is and how God can be discovered and followed. This builds on the twenty-six personal stories of the spiritual discovery of God in his first book.

Where's God? Revelations Today invites us to join in the discovery of God, God's Revelations and inspired messages as we journey towards our own personal and communal salvation with God.

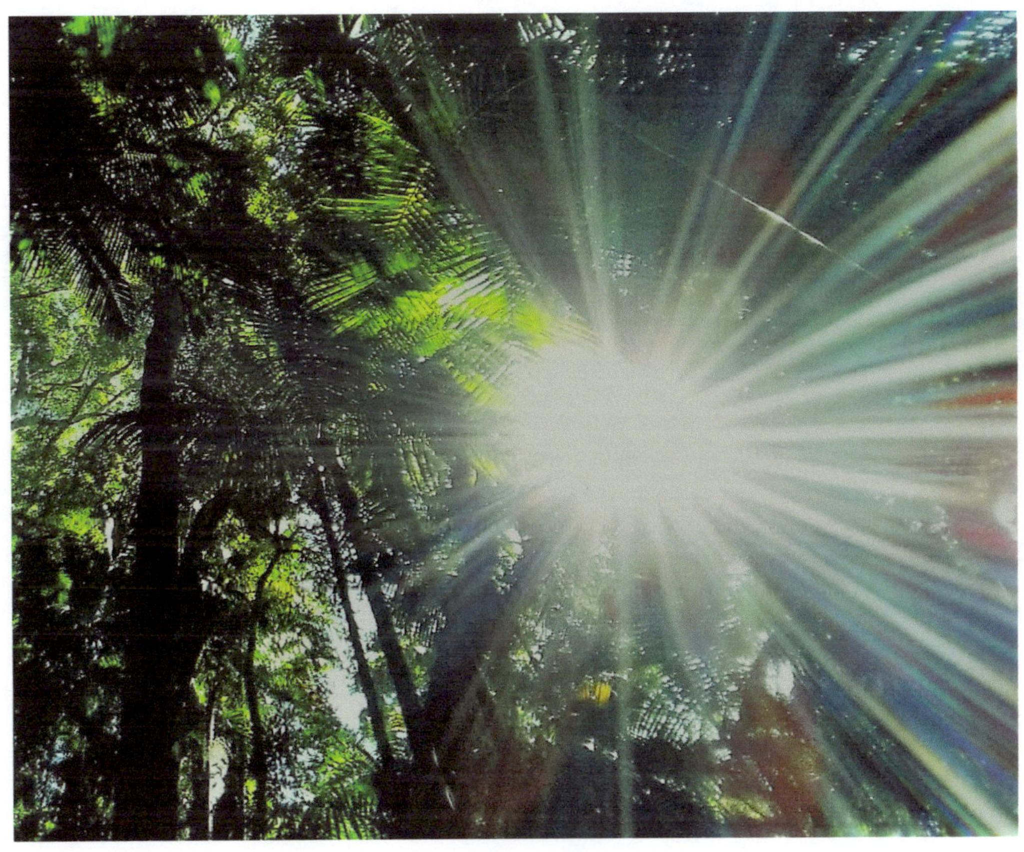

(Karen Foster)
(Karen and Bryan have been married for 40 years.)

Unique Sun Formations

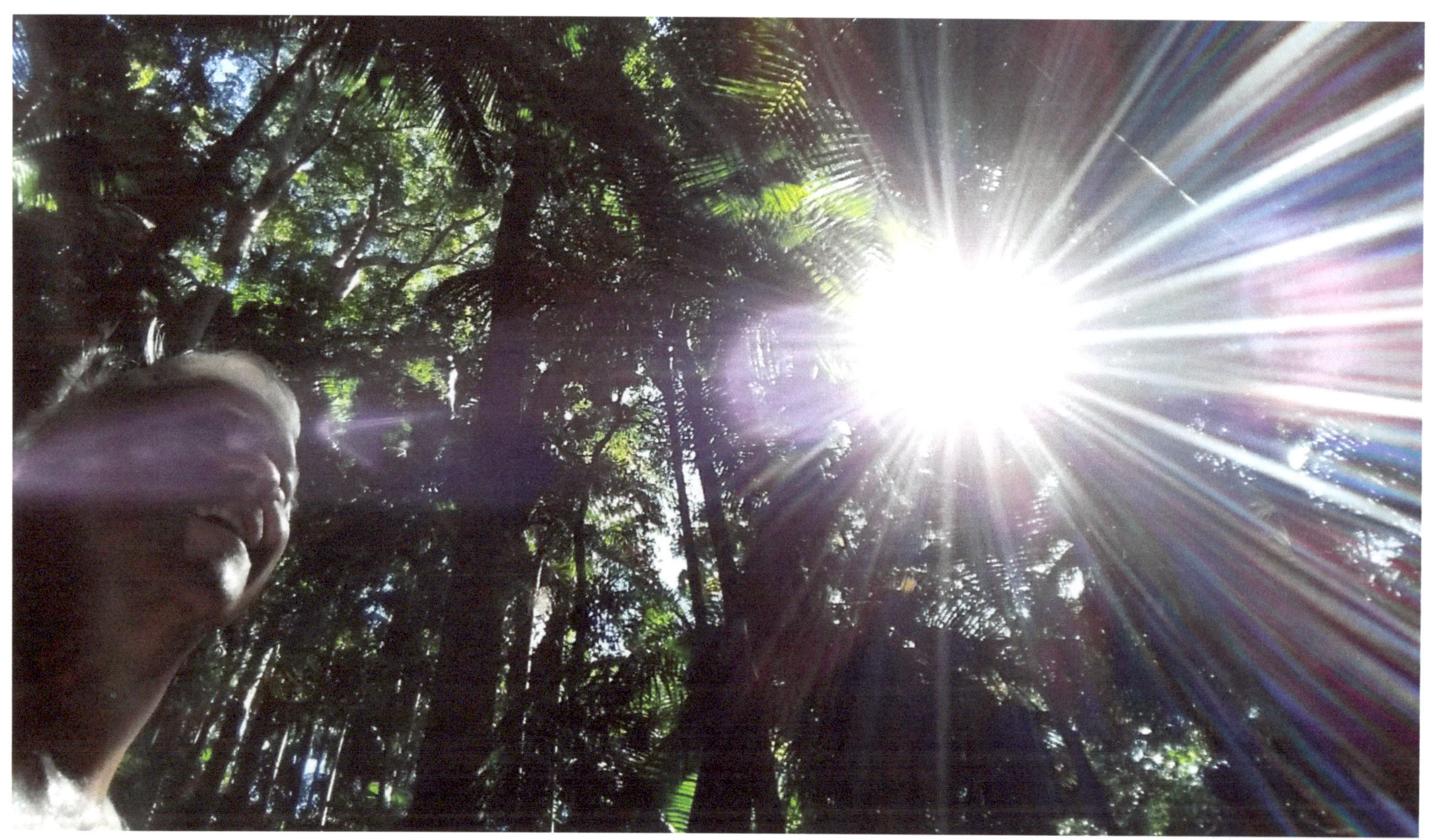

This year there have been quite similar sunlight events to each other, in close time proximity. Two occurred at the foot of Mt Warning just after sunrise months apart, another at Texas on the NSW/Queensland border, while two were at Straddie, North Stradbroke Island, Australia.

The collections of sun images, which occurred this year, are quite spectacular. Each took us by surprise initially. But after considerable contemplation, we realised that God was making a strong point for both Karen and me.

Easter Sun Crosses

The first set of images shared in this photobook show the sun creating the shape of the resurrected sun cross on the weekend after Easter. The resurrected cross developed through these images from a sun ball in the first image to the resurrected cross in the final image. Once again it wasn't apparent while taking the photos. The reality became real afterwards when reviewing the afternoon's shots. These are the most powerful images of something well beyond our capacity to create naturally.

I believe that God's message for us from this set of images is in the death and resurrection of Jesus. The emphasis in the last image is to highlight the truth of the resurrected Jesus as the Christ in Christianity. This series which developed over a few moments is of seven different photographs taken in a similar position towards the sun and is as seen from this rural countryside on the southern side of the Queensland/ New South Wales border at Texas. Being at the end of the week following Easter, the importance of Jesus the Christ is magnified.

There is a challenge here for many religions including Christianity. Even though it is an essential doctrine of Christianity, many question the resurrection's authenticity. There is no doubt whatsoever for me of its reality! It is one reason that God has imaged the sun the way it occurred in these photos. It is God shouting out to us to BELIEVE! But still not forcing us! Jesus is the Christ who rose from the dead and is here with us now through the reality of the Holy Spirit to help guide us towards our salvation.

Texas, on the NSW/Queensland Border

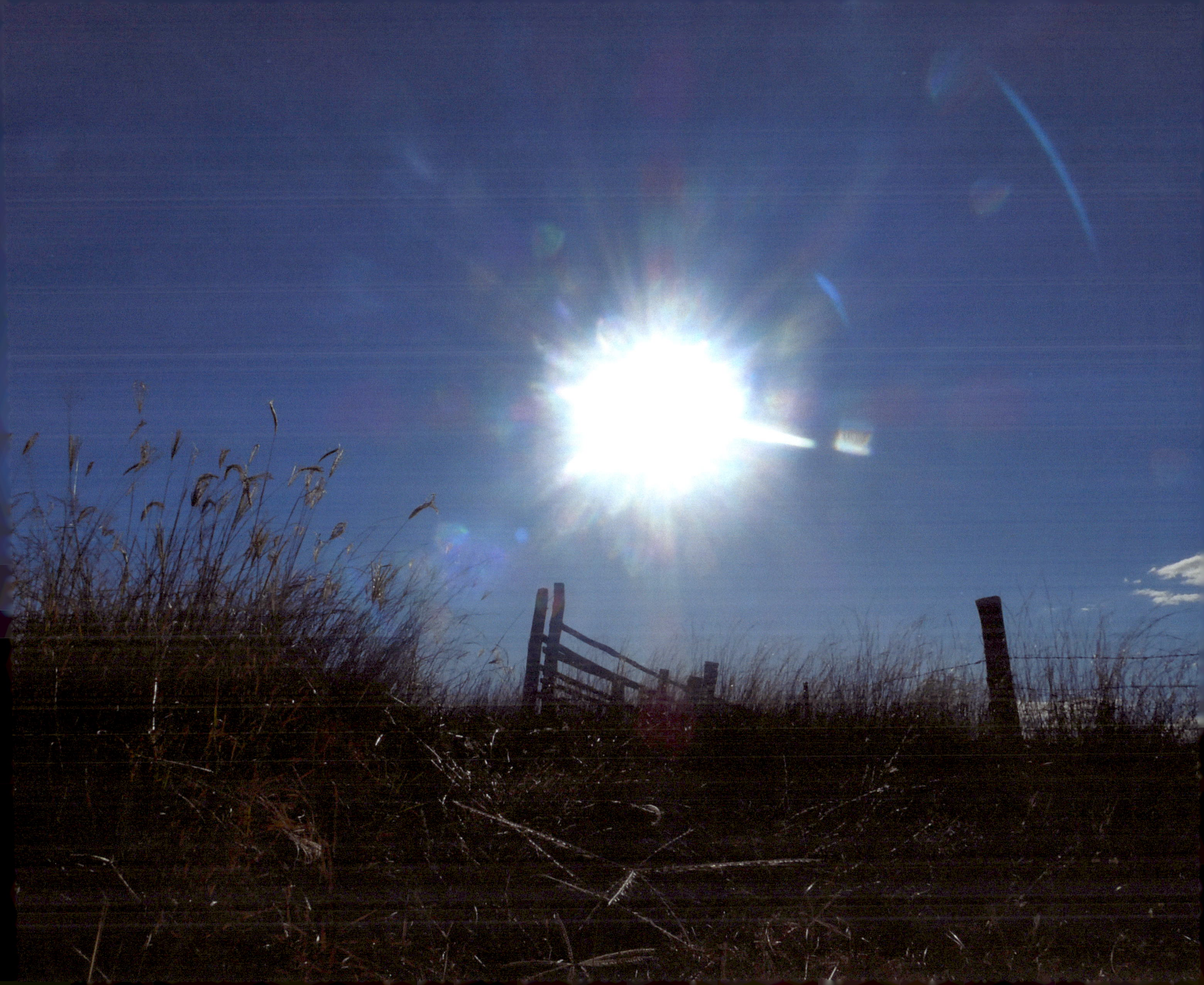

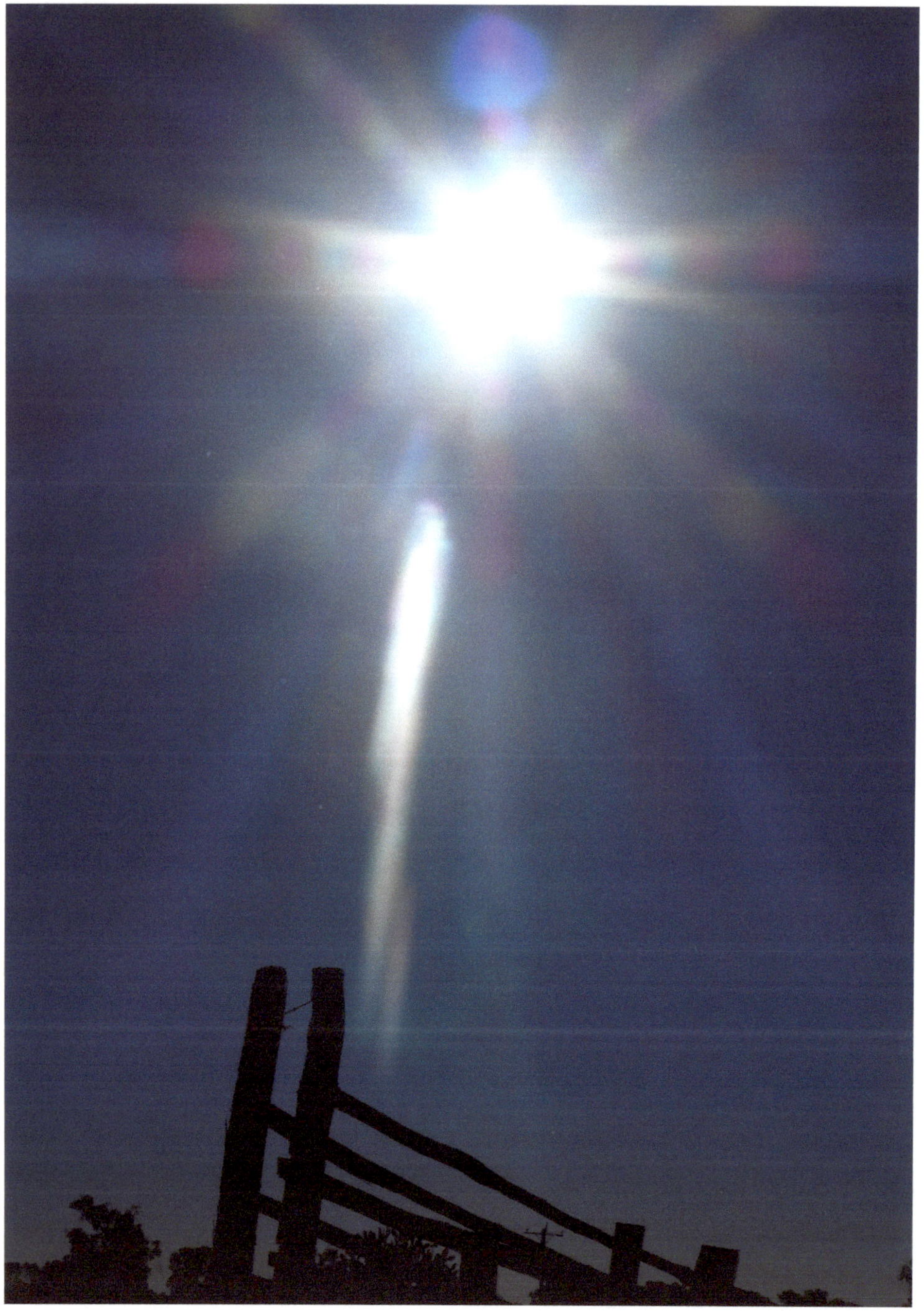

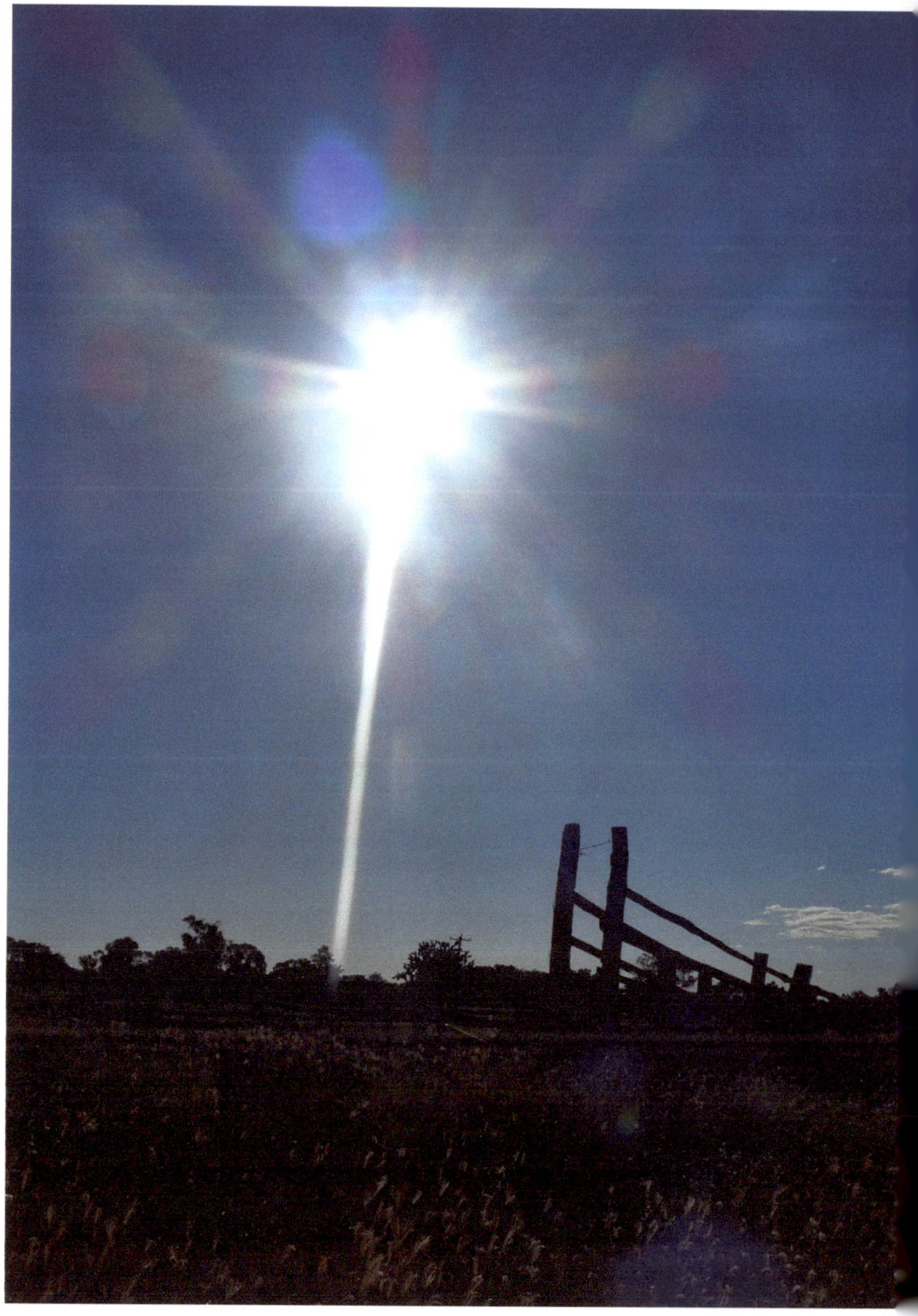

Sun Arrows and Flares

The flares are shown next. These appear to come from the sun and settle on the recipient at the foot of Mt Warning near where the walkers depart for the summit. This only happened on the image and not in reality, as far as I am aware. But as I was the only person there, I am assuming it was only on the image. But who knows?

Once again it is my strong belief that it is a sign from God to believe in what God was passing on. Further explanations are the same as for the sun arrows discussed next.

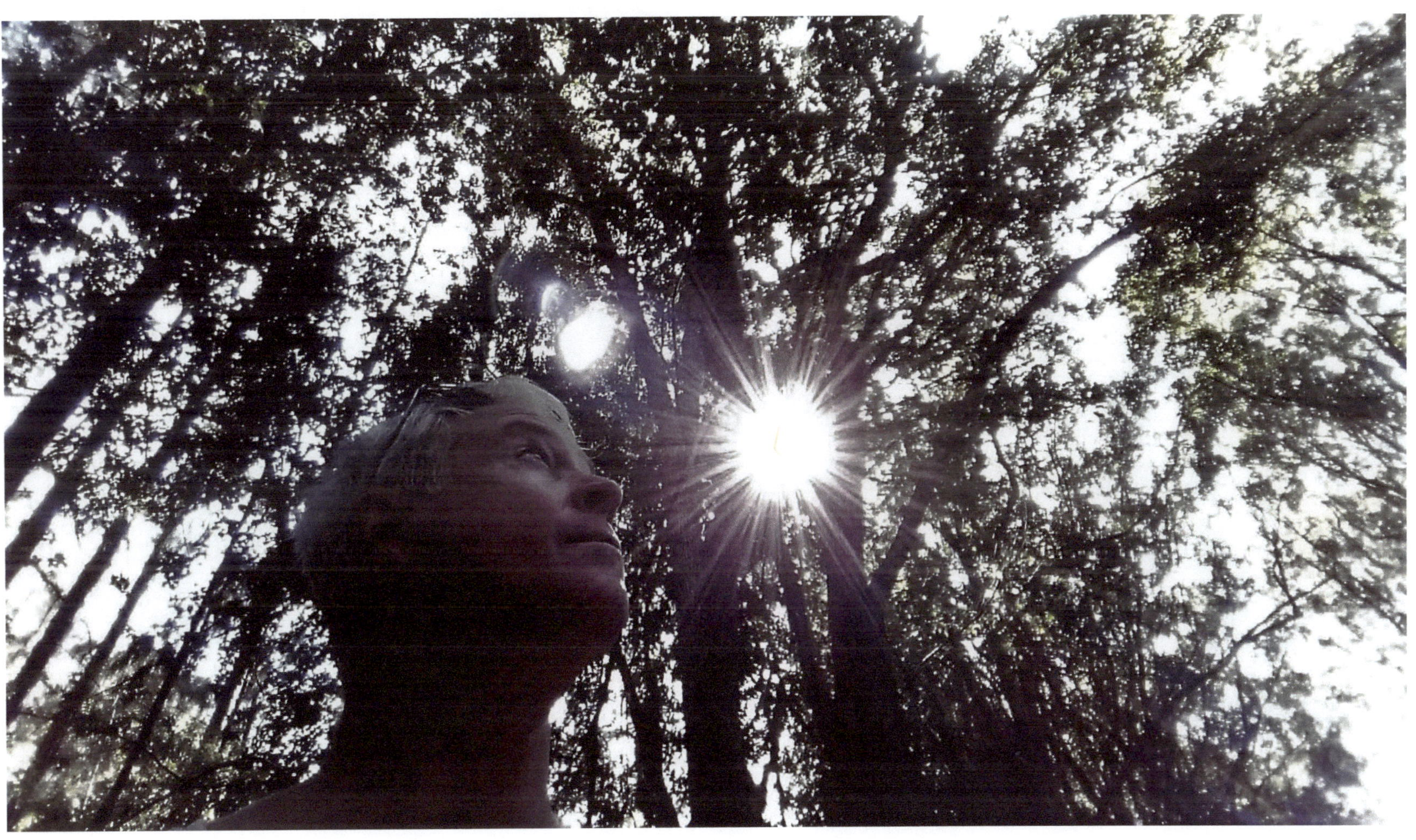

Mt Warning Base

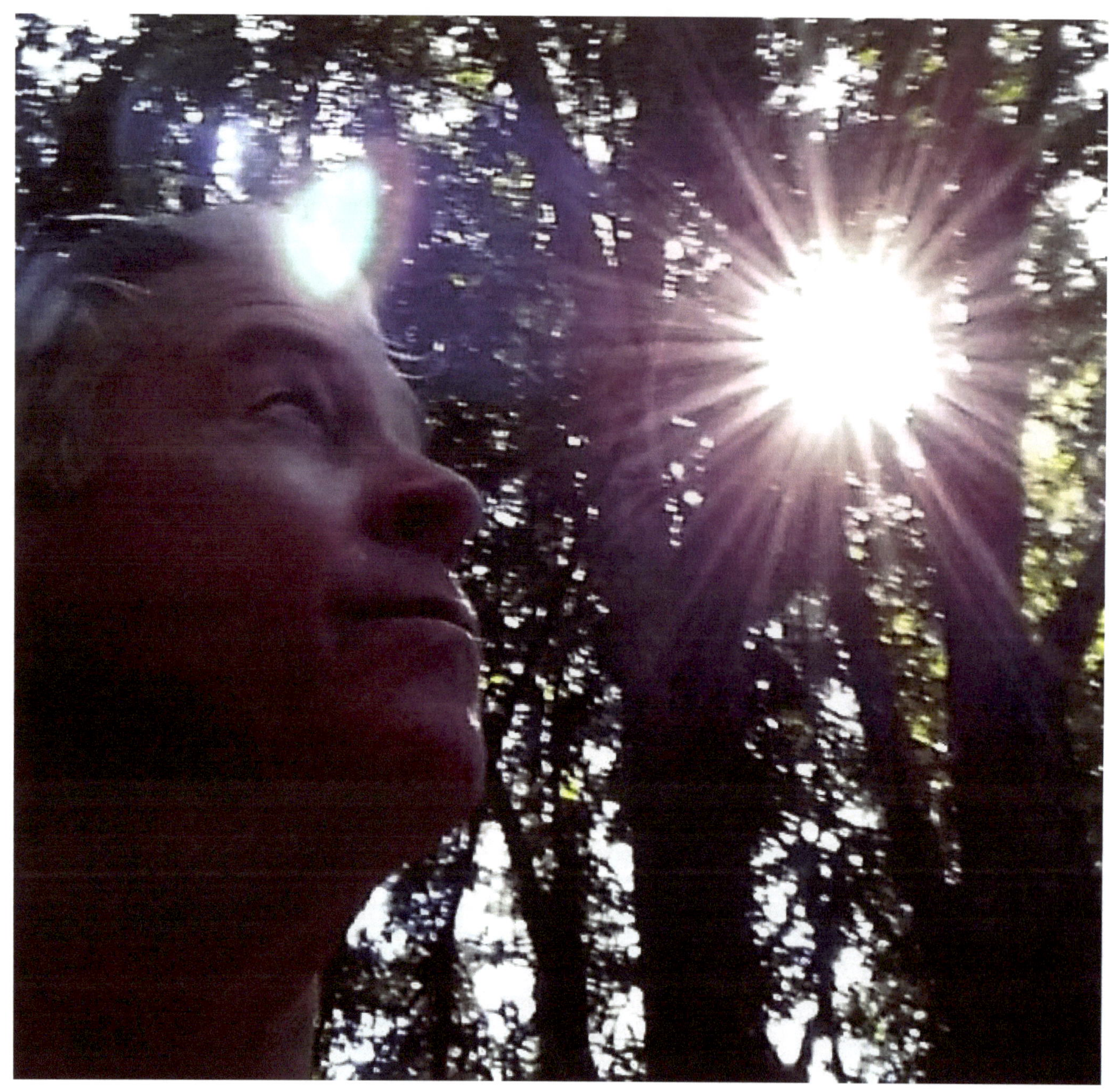

Unique Sun Formations - Authenticity?

Rainforest Canopy Sun and Arrows - WHY?

The first set of images had arrows exploding from the sun, as seen through a rainforest canopy with all its colourful, bright rays and twinkling appearance. The arrows appeared to travel towards me. Each shot had the arrow getting closer until the last one had the arrows becoming one with my head. Extraordinarily though, the photographic images occurred in reverse order. The arrows in image order seem to be going back to the sun.

There will be those who argue that these are just some form of natural reflective or refractive light patterns developed from either the natural surroundings or the camera lenses itself. And this is most likely the case. However, what made these appear is the divine question? God often works through nature and people. It is quite possibly God's way of getting the messages across of God's support and challenges for the recipients.

In other words, this is God's way of doing this supernatural act, naturally.

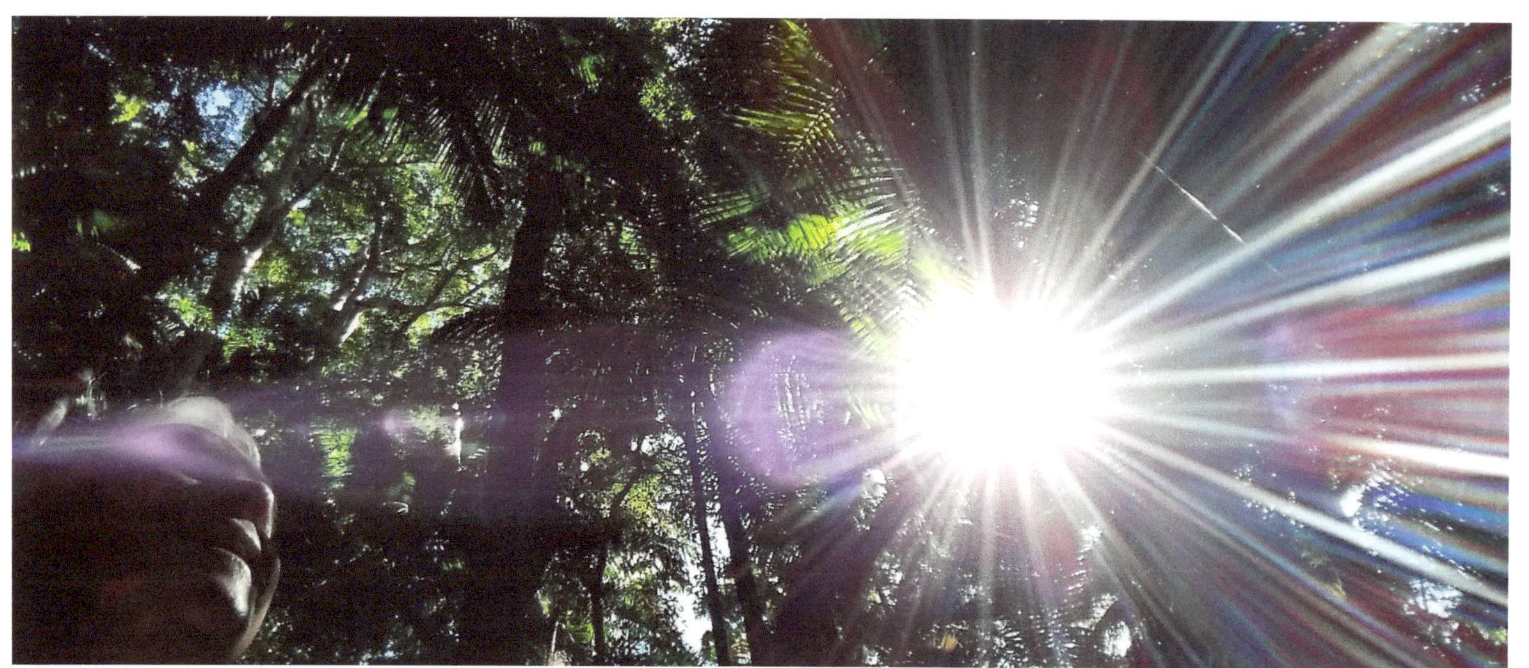

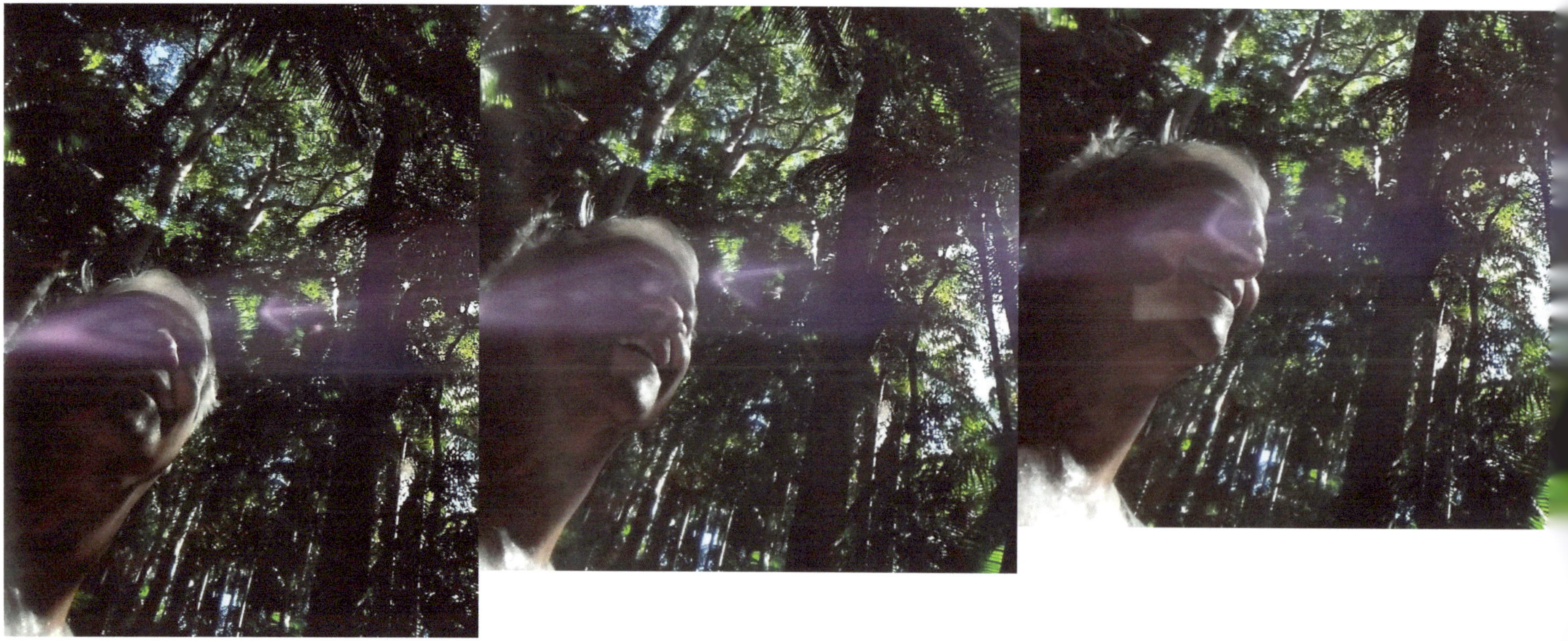

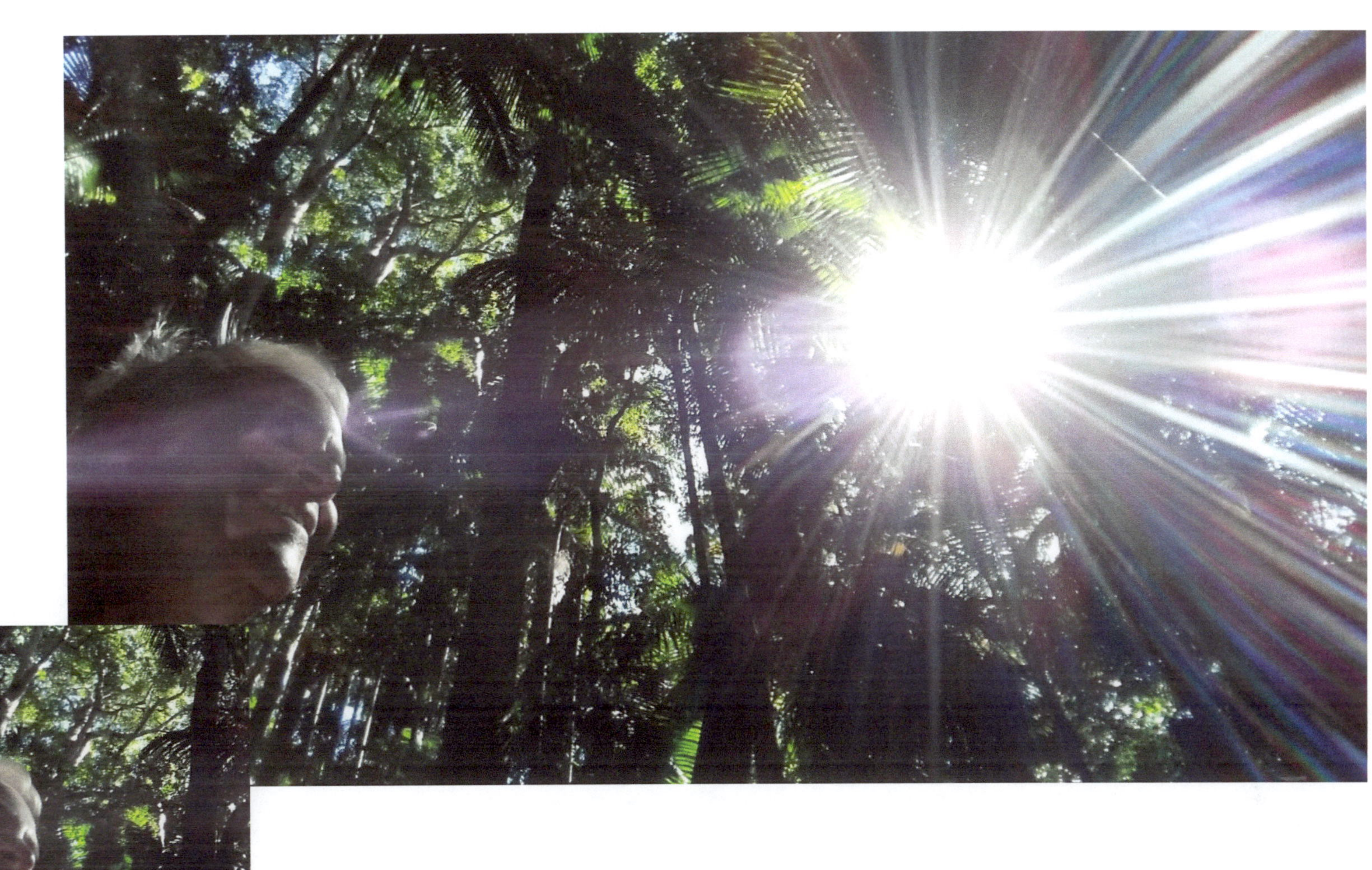

Why would the images appear in reverse order? It is believed that this all comes back to the appreciation of God's Free Will for each of us. God never forces a belief in God or God's actions on anyone. Each person, out of the absolute love of God for us, must decide for him/herself what is true and what is not. Absolute love from God requires absolute freedom from the recipient. Otherwise, it is not absolute love. (p153)

Therefore, if these images of the arrow coming from the sun, a metaphor for God, was as seen and in actual order, it places a high degree of necessity on the receiver to believe it literally as a way for God to make the point. God won't make a point of faith so strongly to anyone that it must be believed without choice! Placing the order of the photographs backwards places doubt as to their meaning or accuracy in the mind of the receiver. The necessity to believe is gone. There now appears an act of faith necessary to believe the message and to then act upon it. We must remember that we have no right to put God to the test.

Are the arrows to be taken literally as God pointing to me for a reason? Or maybe God coming to me? Or maybe metaphorically, as the messages moving from God to me?

What is the message then? Is it that God is highlighting that there are many important messages that I need to get out to the world? That after all my religious training, living, prayer, meditation, teaching, reflection and action now requires me to go out into the world and spread God's revelations and messages? After all, God has passed on these revelations and messages to me over the past fifty years or so. A concentration has occurred in the past few years. Is this an aspect that occurs as one gets older, hopefully wiser, and hence the need to share this outward, just as the sun rays did and do?

When these are combined with God's other methods of telling me of something important, particularly the 'Tears from God', which appear at those special encounter moments, you know that there is something of importance to be aware of, e.g. a revelation or an inspired message from God.

When contemplating these photos and discussing these with Karen, Tears from God answered the question of authenticity. The images were truly from God. I was asked to pass on those Revelations and messages which I had received over decades, especially those in need within our world today.

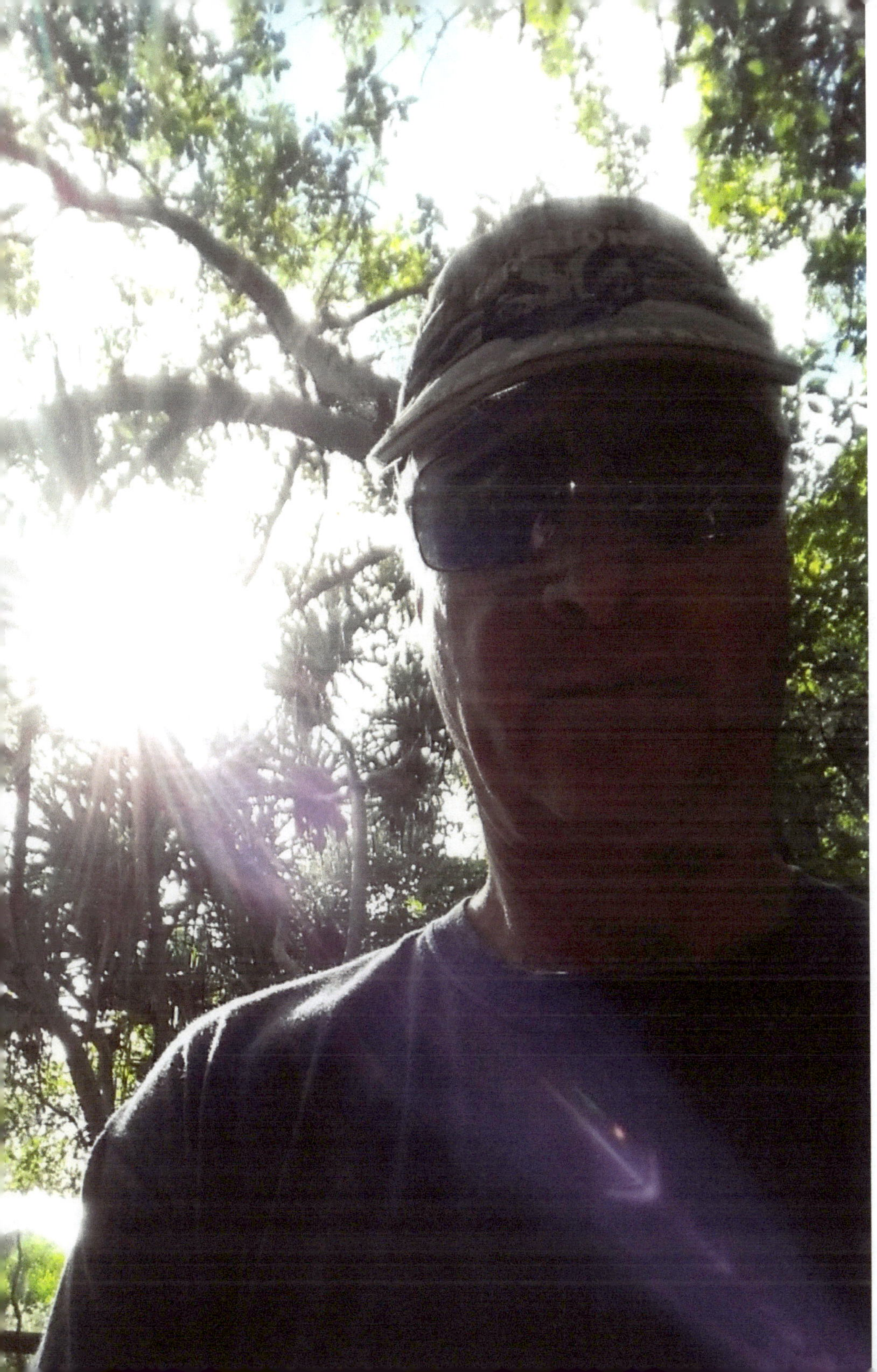

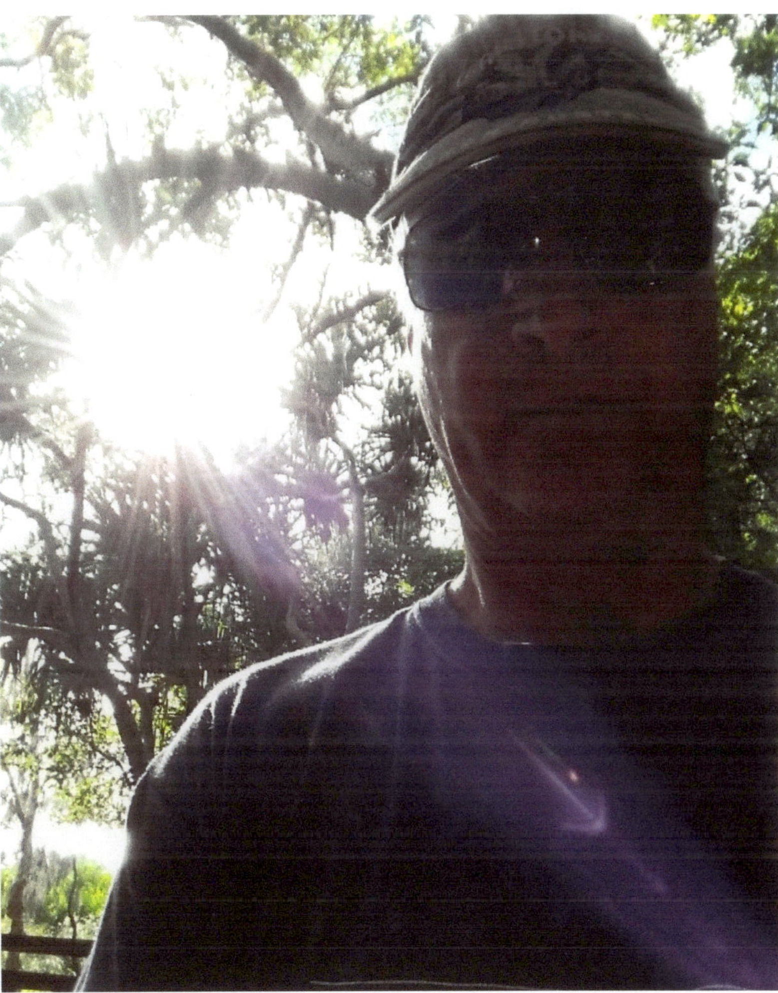

**Cylinder Beach,
North Stradbroke Island**

Straddie sun arrows + double rainbow

Another set of seven arrow images was taken, this time on 27 May 2018 while at Cylinder Beach, North Stradbroke Island, off Brisbane, Australia. It was coincidentally on the second anniversary of the receival of the six inspired messages from God while on the plains of Mt Warning in 2016. These arrows created the same appearance as travelling from the sun to the recipient. Each appears to travel towards the heart and then be consumed.

Later that afternoon there appeared a double rainbow above the caravan/trailer. I only became aware of this occurrence when something inside made me go across the park's roadway and look backwards. The magnificence then hit me. I was able to get some images of this rainbow, but these appeared so inadequate compared to the actual source. The significance of this event certainly challenged me. Once again on the second anniversary of the six inspired messages from God. These messages were originally received while I was sitting outside this same van. And the van was the venue where during the following night two years ago I received God's Revelations. The van is very significant in the experiences of the Revelation and inspired messages. Was this God once again highlighting the reality and the Truth of these revelatory experiences of two years ago? I think so.

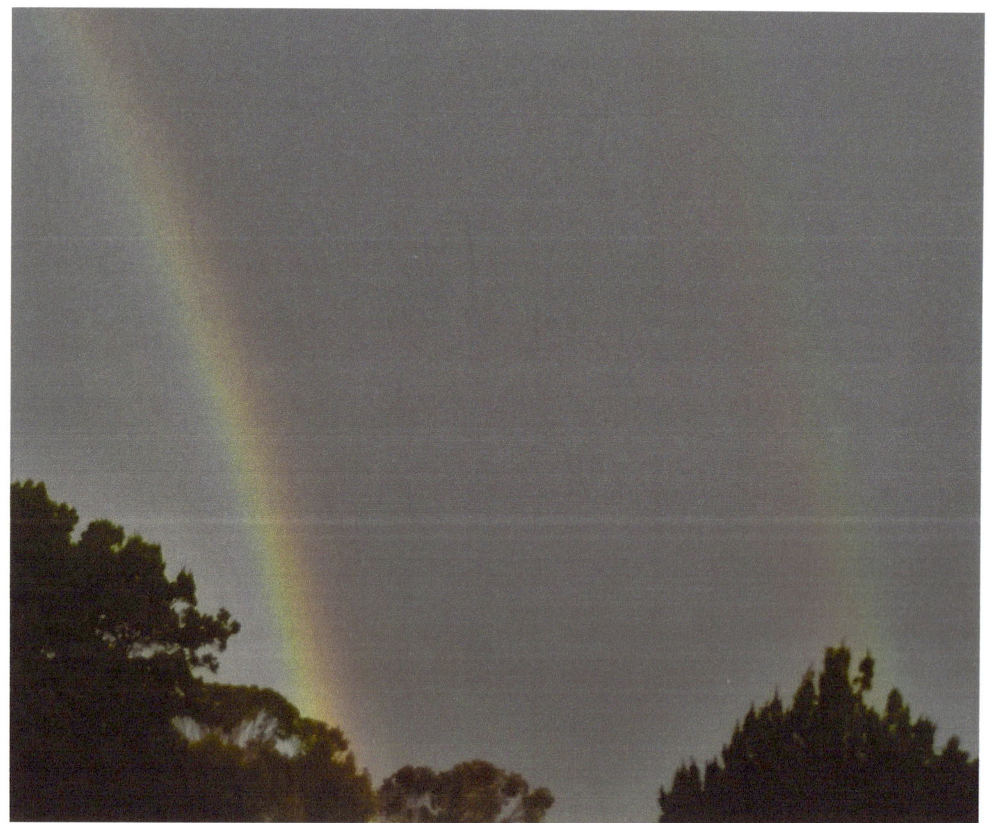

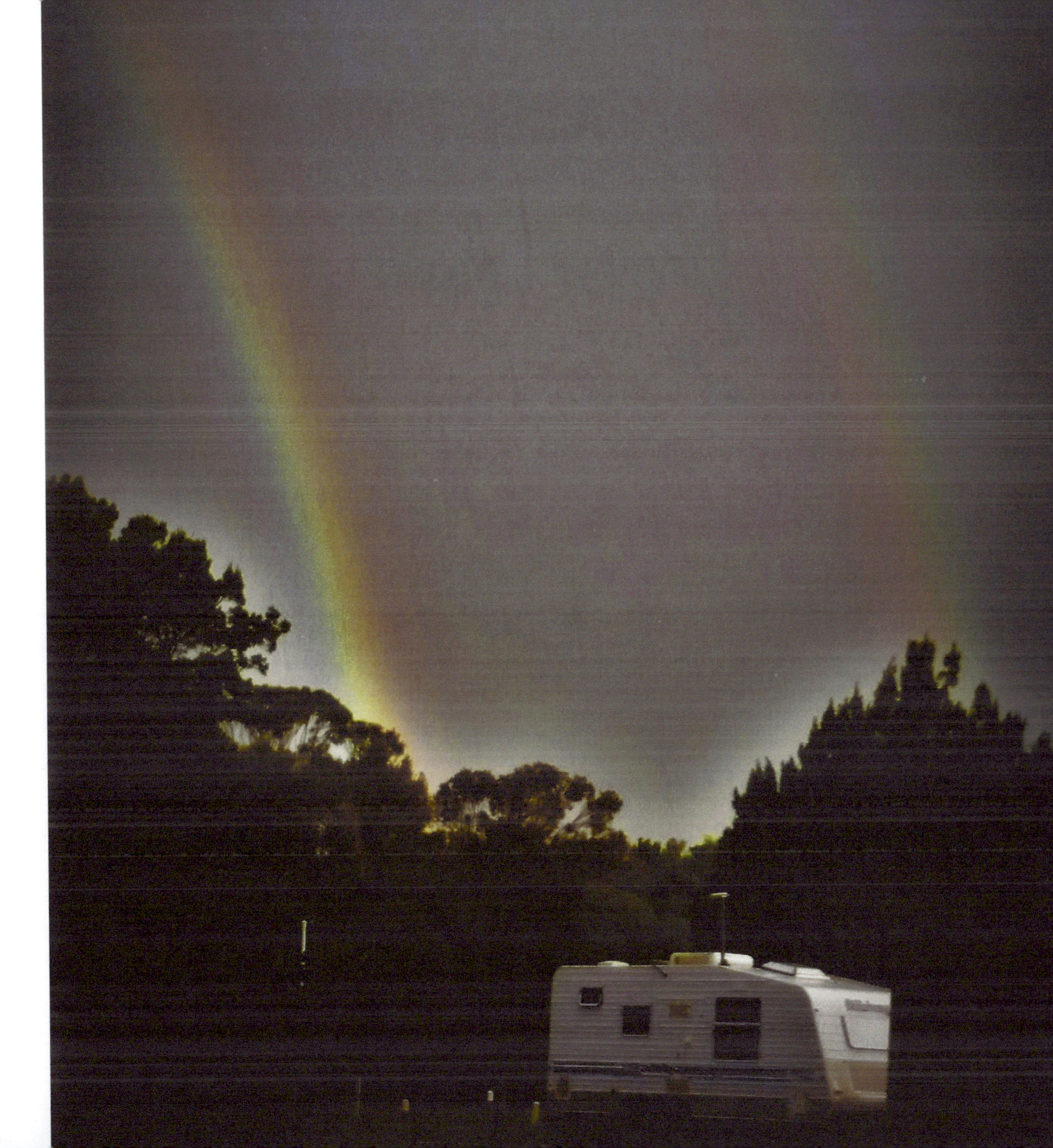

Mt Warning Cloud – Rays Shooting Outwards

Last year a small cloud was positioned immediately on top of the peak of Mt Warning when viewed from the north. It was reminiscent of 'God coming to the mountain' as is often noted in various scriptures.

This wasn't all though. When viewed closely, rays were emanating from the cloud outwards. Why such a magnificent scene? It is believed to be another sign pointing to the significance of the mountain. It was the first physical sign in the sky that I was aware of and that appeared to be from God, especially in the biblical sense. No doubt it was directed towards all those who saw this image and interpreted it accordingly. Otherwise, for other observers, it was just a very special image worth remembering.

Once again the sunlight was somehow being used by God to make an inspired point. I believe it was to highlight the significance and magnificence of Mt Warning for God in making a series of Revelations and inspired messages known.

As a consequence of this, for me, it was to be aware of Mt Warning's significance to God, so as to believe in the authenticity of the gifts from God, i.e. God's Revelations and inspired messages received at its foot and on its plains.

As well, it emphasised God's support for me to reveal these to others.

(*Where's God? Revelations Today*, Bryan Foster, 2018, Great Developments Publishers, Gold Coast, p147-162)

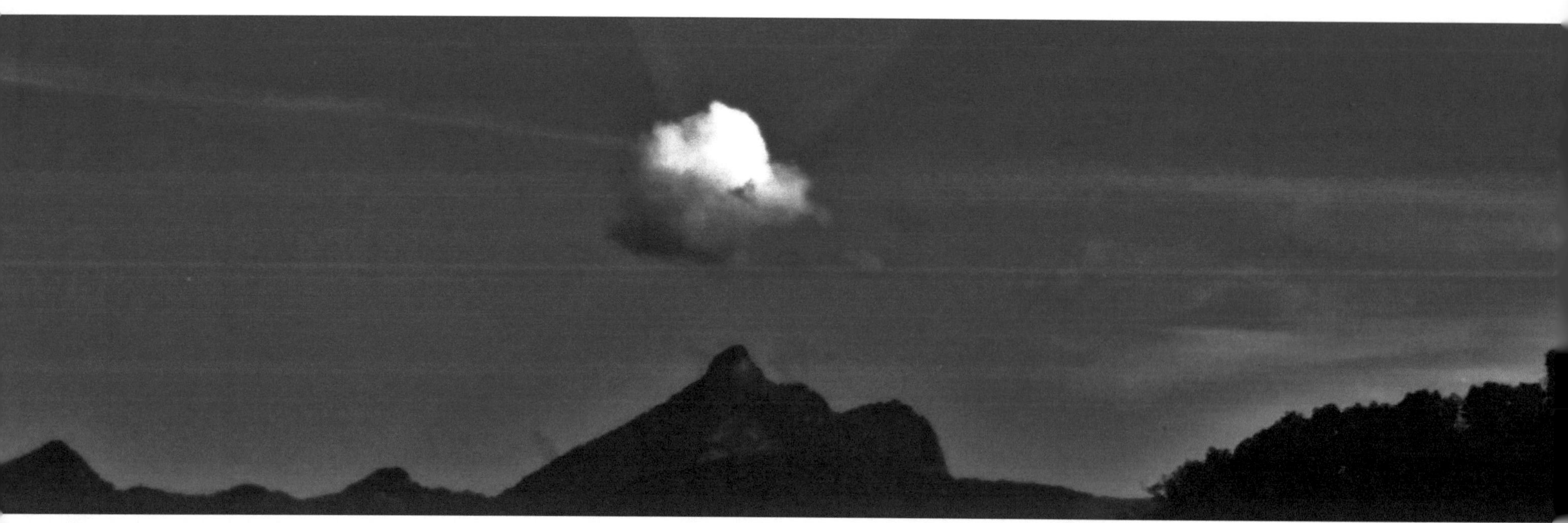

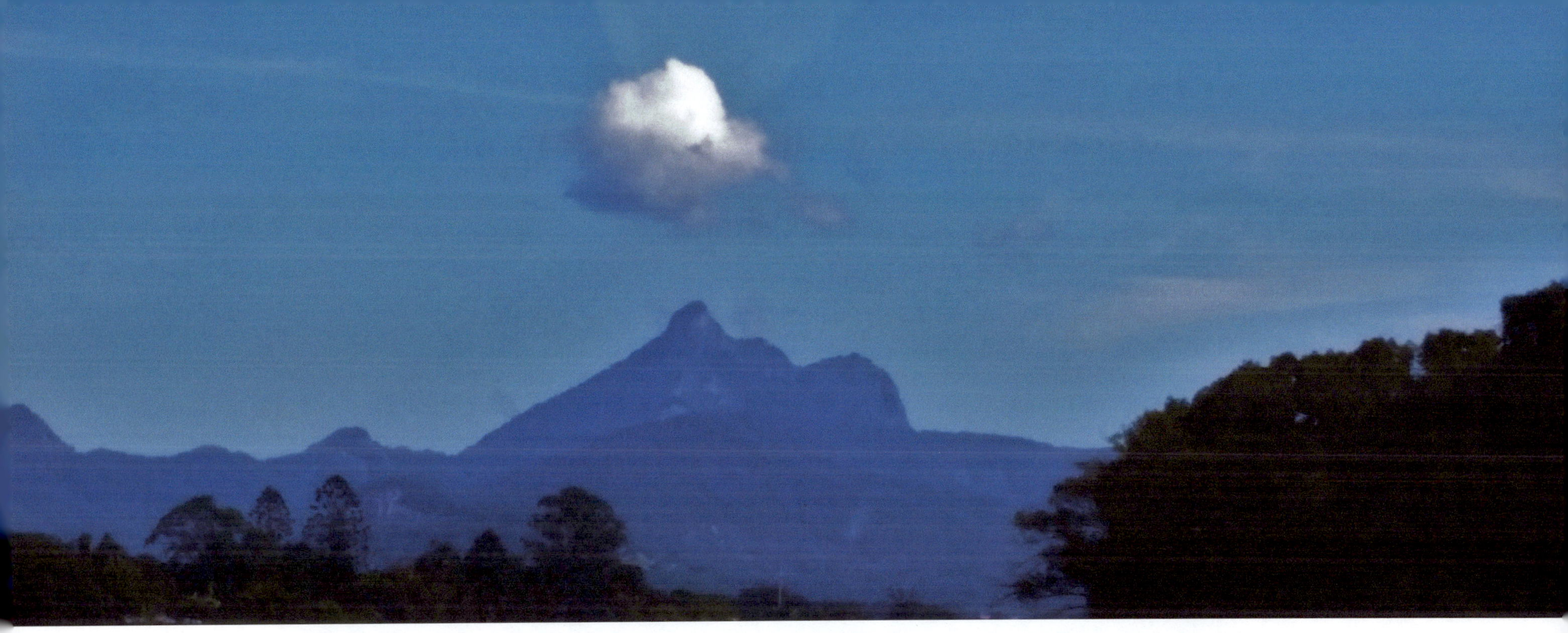

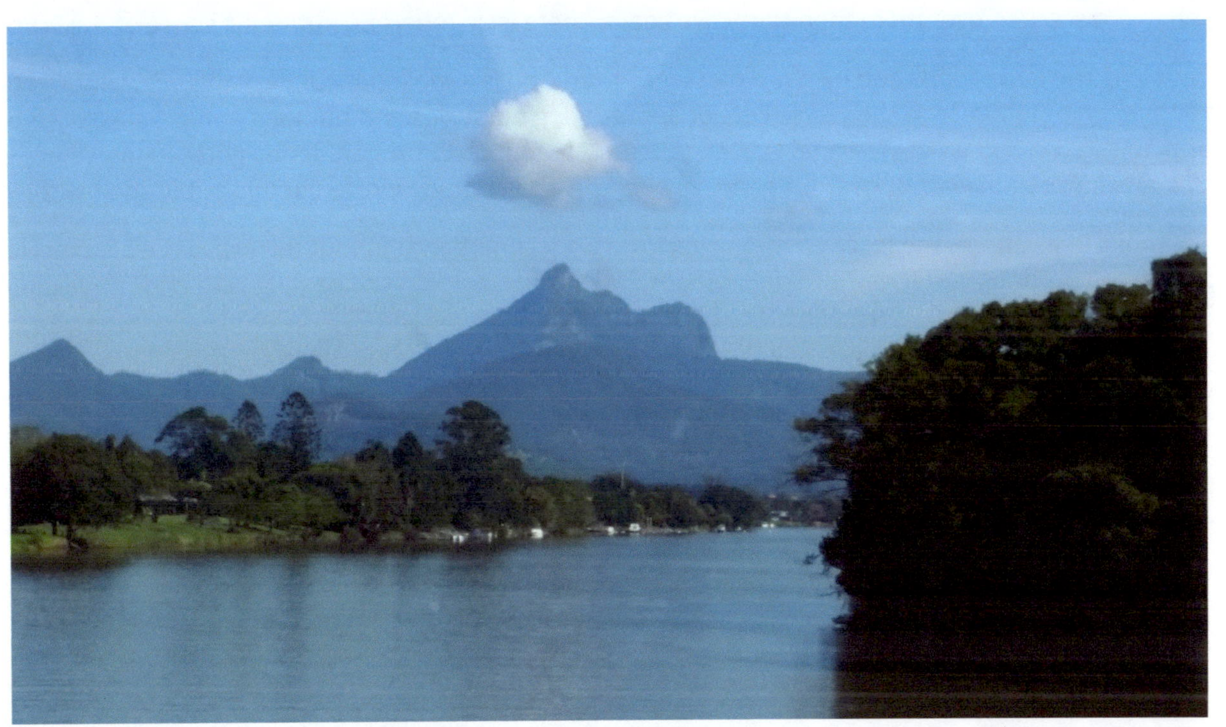

25

Revelations and Inspired Messages from God

Background

The concept of 'Revelations' in this book is also referred to as 'Special or Direct Revelations' in various religious circles in society. These Revelations are specifically directed by God to individuals or groups. What is referred to as 'inspired messages' in this publication may, at times, be referred to as 'General Revelations' in other religious publications and discussions? These are from God to anyone in general, being received through such means as nature, ethical appreciations and cognitive reasoning. (GCSE, BBC) Christianity believes that Jesus is the ultimate example of the fullness of Revelation observed on this earth by humanity. (Oxford Scholarship, 2018) The different religions have various appreciations of the relevance of Revelations historically and today. All genuine religions believe that God reveals Godself to this world through various forms, especially through people, their beliefs and morality, and through the natural world.

The terms 'Revelation' and 'inspired messages' are used as points of clarity. Naming every message with which God inspires humanity with the term 'Revelation' may become confusing as there are different levels of Revelation. 'Revelation' is used when there is direct contact of God with specific people, while 'inspired messages' are for those revelations discerned by people as emanating from God. How both of these occur is explained.

This book is primarily about explaining the various Revelations I received directly from God in 1982 and 2016, along with the inspired messages received from God and discerned over more than thirty-five years. There is an inherent, authentic sense of the Truth being shared.

As an author, extolling the Revelations and inspired messages from God is a most difficult task. It goes well beyond just writing some thoughts and meanings. It goes to the whole core of appreciating ourselves and humanity and our association with God. To claim the authority to do so is a massive personal challenge. Rest assured it hasn't been done lightly. In fact, there is considerable truly heartfelt anxiety. In my heart of hearts, I genuinely believe in everything written in this publication wholeheartedly.

The collection is one author's Revelations and inspired messages from God. Others throughout the world are also receiving Revelations and inspired messages. Some will probably put these into publications. We all have our ways of dealing with and propagating what we receive. All people can receive God's messages and Revelations. The big question for each person is, Am I ready and open to receiving messages or Revelations from God? Would I know when I received any? What would I do with these if and when I had similar experiences? God inspires us in so many ways, particularly through other people and nature. Am I aware of inspired messages from God through others and our world?

These Revelations and inspired messages revealed to me have been developing over at least forty years. It is not something which has just eventuated.

Justification

The key reasons for believing that these Revelations and inspired messages are from God will be explained in more detail. The specific reasons follow. Each reason is explained in detail in the *Where's God? Revelations Today* textbook.

- the 25th birthday experience of God in May 1982;

- the longevity without any personal doubt of this strong association with God;

- the Tears from God experiences, which have been growing in intensity and frequency, especially in the most recent years;

- the Revelations from God at the foot of Mt Warning in May 2016;

- **the recent photographic images highlighting metaphorical or direct links with God;**

- **coincidences and signs from God over many years**

- the personal career/vocation, 40 years teaching religion from years 1-12, including 30 years of Study of Religion to senior years;

- holding senior leadership positions in religious schools and parishes;

- prayer and meditation throughout and

- the continued strong support and agreement from my wife, Karen.

Each of these reasons supports the belief in either the Revelation or inspired messages being from God. God never forces anyone to believe anything. There is a level of 'proof' but also the mystery of the faith with any Revelation or inspired message from God. Therefore, it is through the combinations of these reasons and others, that God's special presence is experienced with the outcomes of each needed to be shared. Having always been close to God, or at least in my teens on the fringes, allows for that openness to hear and know intrinsically when something is legitimately from God.

GCSE BBC, http://www.bbc.co.uk/schools/gcsebitesize/rs/god/chrevelationrev1.shtml

Oxford Scholarship Online, Jesus the Fullness of Revelation, http://www.oxfordscholarship.com/view/10.1093/acprof:oso/9780199605569.001.0001/acprof-9780199605569-chapter-5

(*Where's God? Revelations Today*, Bryan Foster, 2018, Great Developments Publishers, Gold Coast, p35-45)

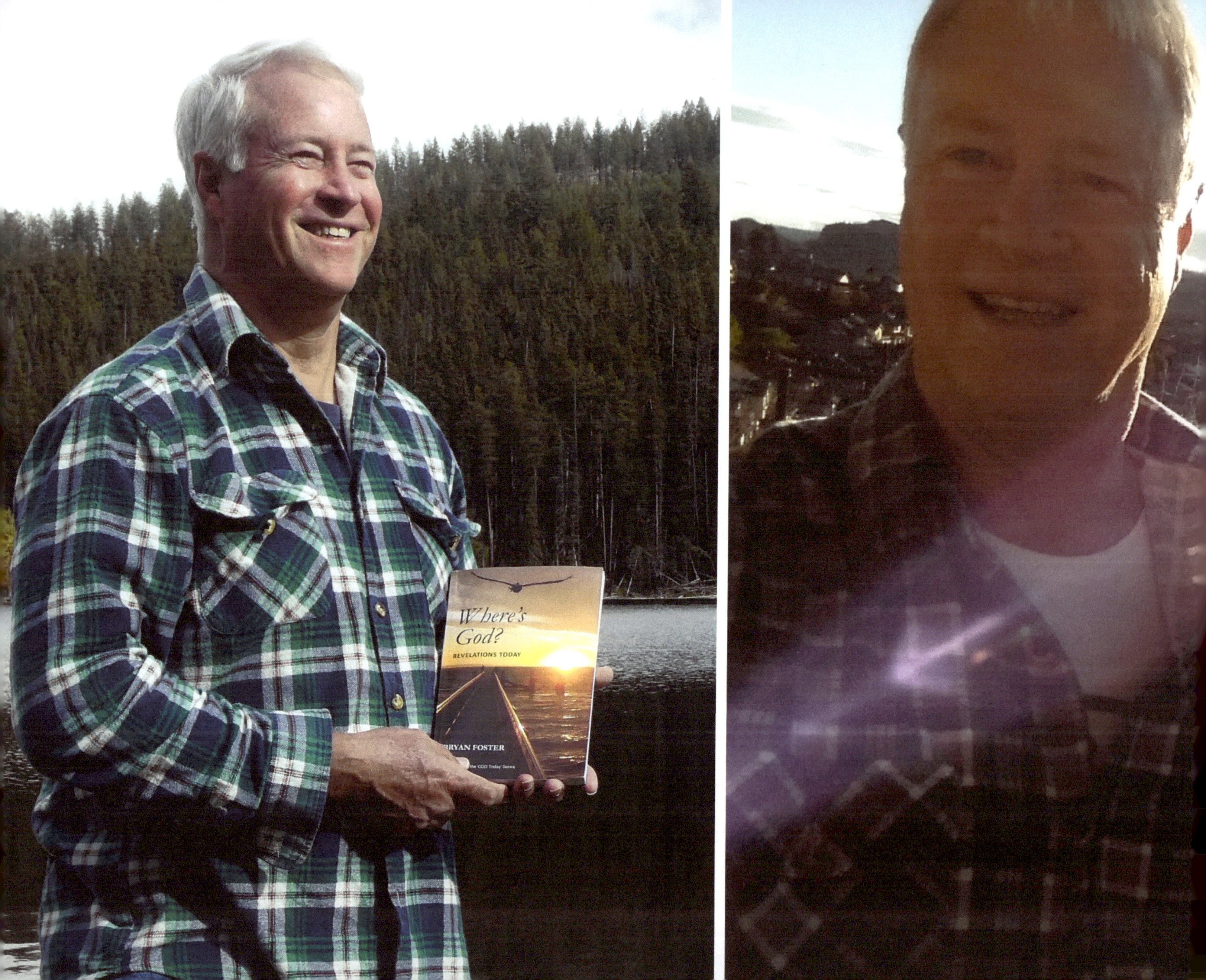
Where's
God?
REVELATIONS TODAY
BRYAN FOSTER
the GOD Today Series

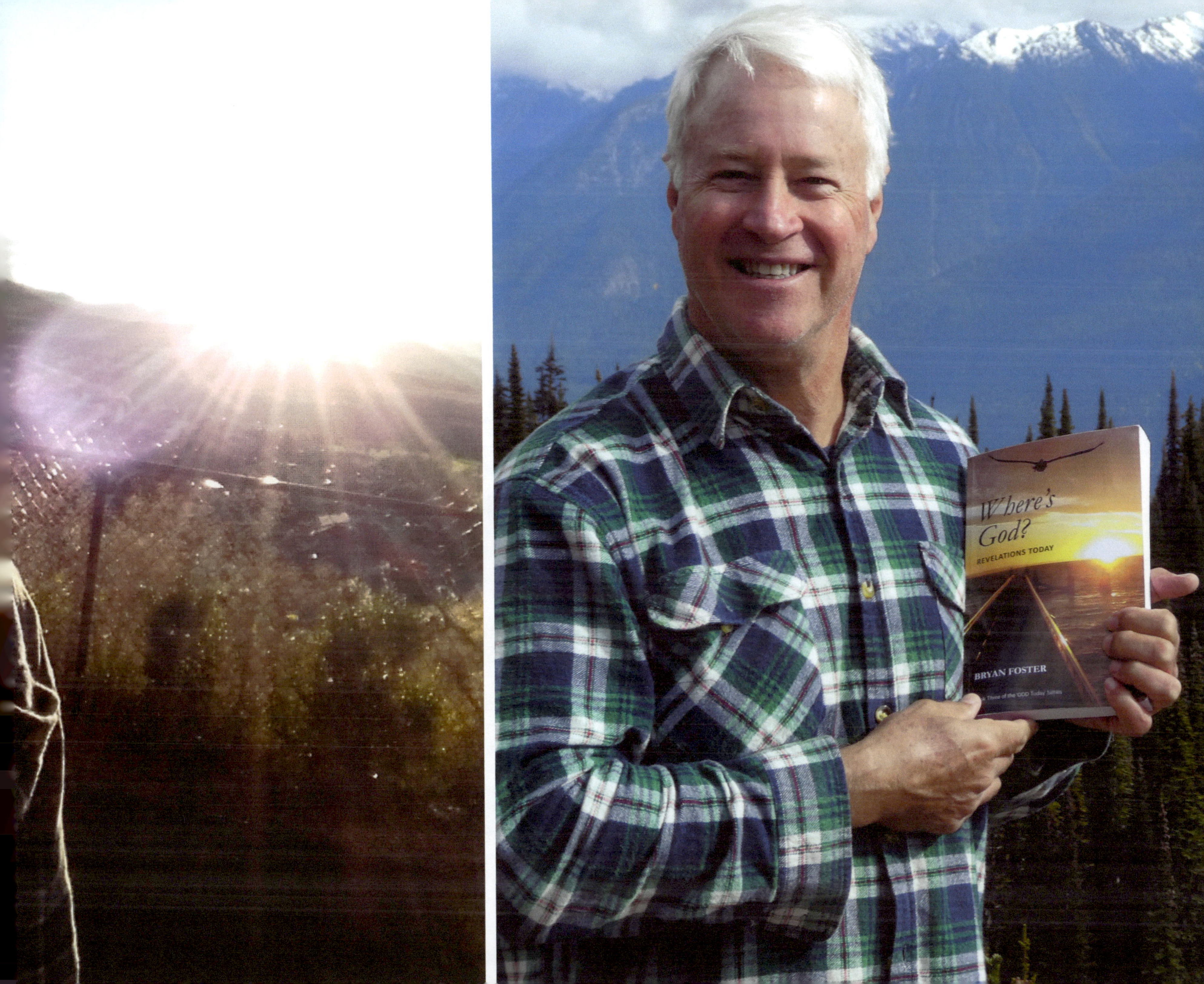
Where's
God?
REVELATIONS TODAY
BRYAN FOSTER

God's Revelations

God's Revelations were received in the freshness of the cool early morning night at Murwillumbah Showgrounds on the foot of Mt Warning, Australia, 28 May 2016.

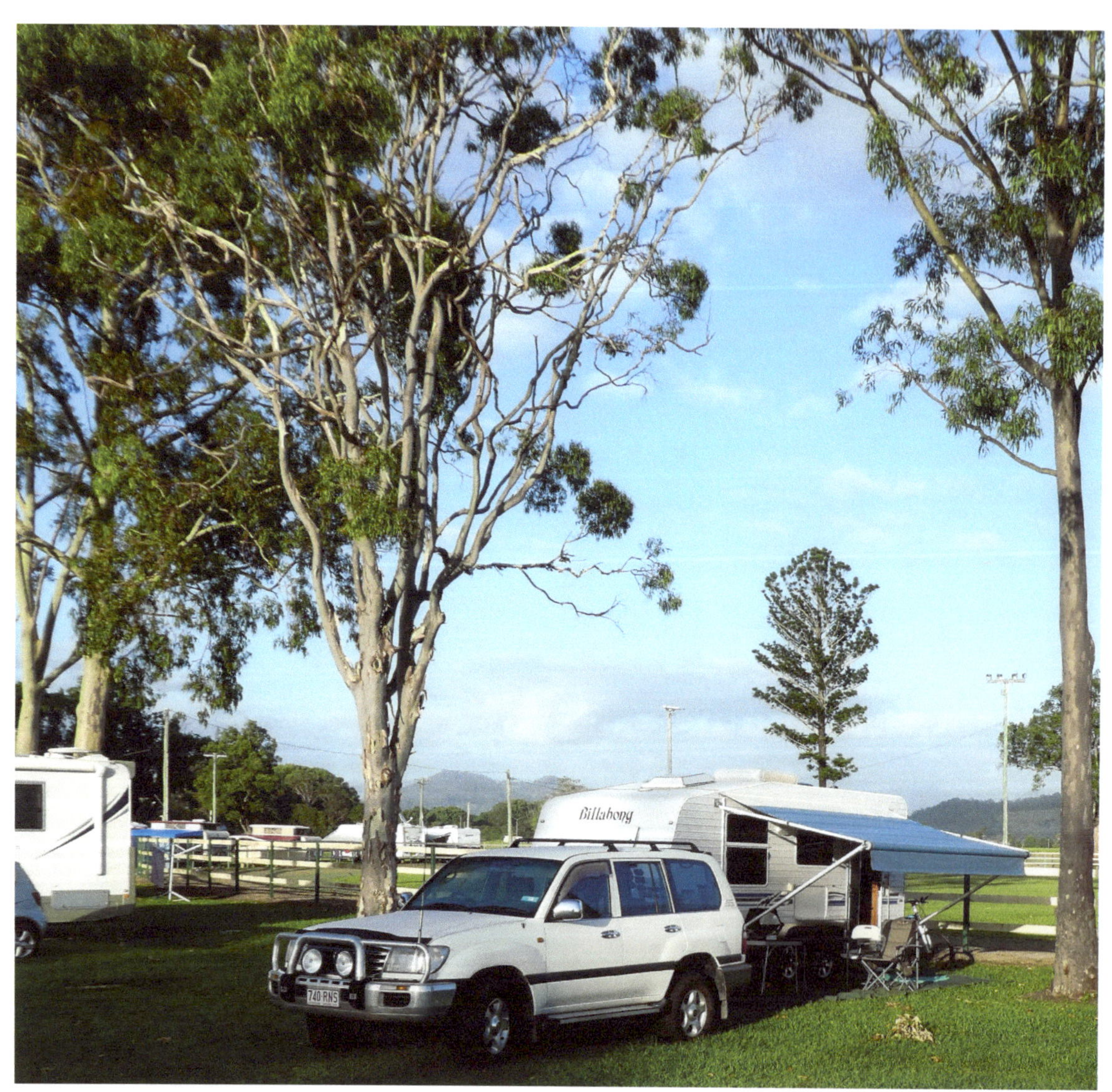

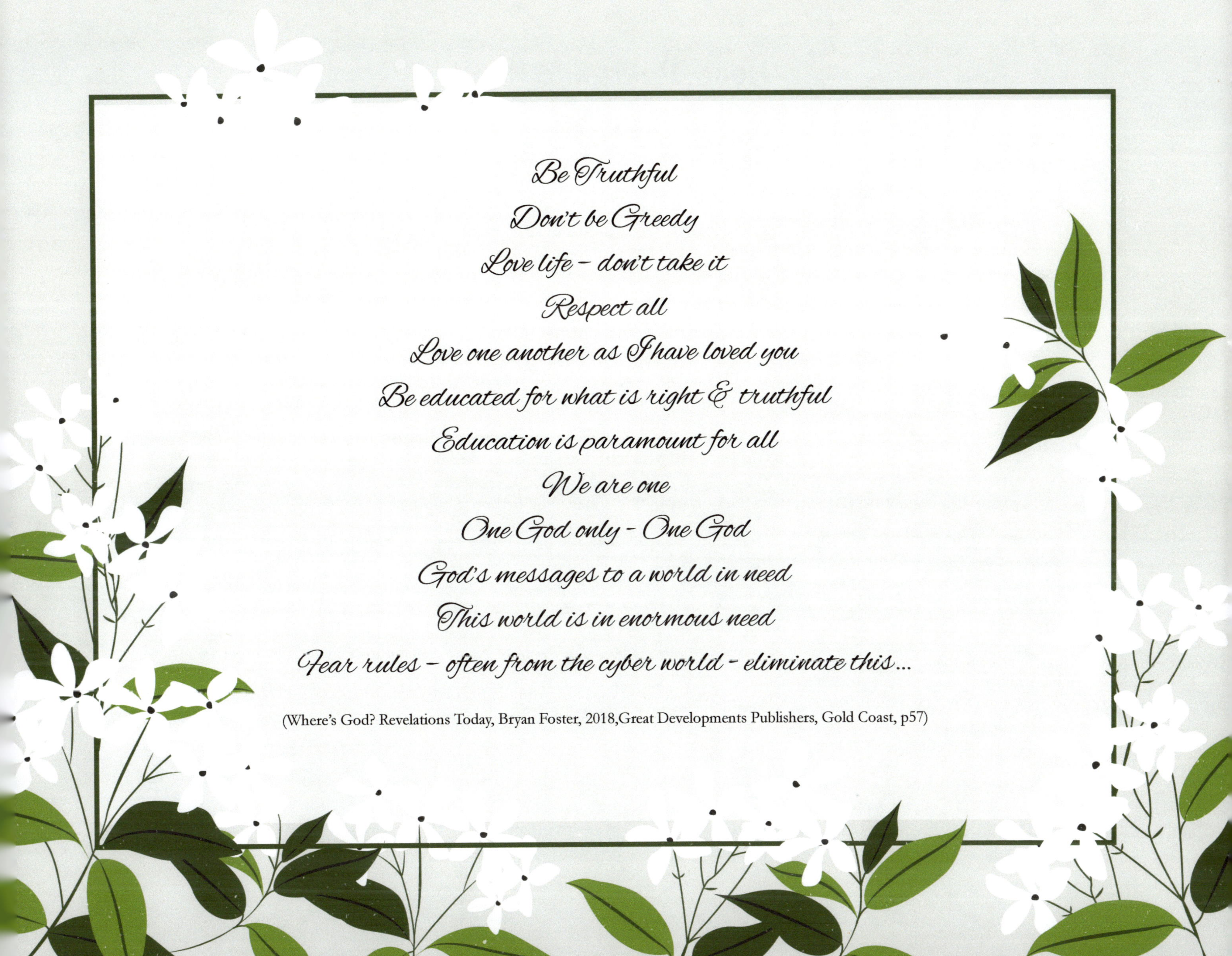

Be Truthful

Don't be Greedy

Love life – don't take it

Respect all

Love one another as I have loved you

Be educated for what is right & truthful

Education is paramount for all

We are one

One God only – One God

God's messages to a world in need

This world is in enormous need

Fear rules – often from the cyber world – eliminate this…

(Where's God? Revelations Today, Bryan Foster, 2018,Great Developments Publishers, Gold Coast, p57)

Head, Heart and Hands

Interestingly, the unique sun arrows which appeared to fly at and through me flew towards two features – the head on the first morning and then the heart some weeks later. Could this be significant? Various religious groups see the significance of the head, heart and hands. Each symbolises something special. The head is the intellect and the decision maker, the heart is the lifeblood, feelings and emotions, while the hands stand for the response and the doing aspects.

In this particular case, it seems that the arrows were highlighting a couple of key components needed to espouse God's recently received Revelations and inspired messages. Both the intellect and decision making were needed to know and appreciate the facts and key messages received, while the emotions of what is involved with receiving these and needing to teach/live these became apparent.

It became a case of there being some options and which did I wish to pursue. The easiest was to ignore these Revelations and inspired messages or just put everything in the too hard basket. With options right through to writing, publishing, presenting, marketing, promoting and living each one. The initial reaction was one of firstly being so honoured for this to have occurred. Then being an author, it felt so obviously correct to write about it. This grew into seeing it as being an essential need. The option taken was to pursue this, and it became the *1God.world: One God for All* publication.

The book was published, marketed and lived. A follow-up book of photos was produced the following year to enhance the written word, *Mt Warning God's Revelations: Photobook Companion to 1God.world.* During this whole process, it became more and more apparent how difficult it was going to be both professionally and personally. How far did I want to pursue this? (Elsewhere in the new book this is explained further. See *Where's God? Revelations Today*)

Where did the hands fit into this scenario? Being selfie images, the hands were required to take the photos. Hence, they didn't appear in any of the images. Yet these hands were integral to the whole process. I would like to think that the hands, symbolising the response and the doing of the received Revelation and messages, stood for everything that followed the receival on that afternoon and night two years ago. Everything from writing both books, publishing these across various platforms, developing websites, promoting the books' sales, delivering copies to various stores, taking photos for the photobook and websites, developing promotional and informative videos of the mountain and what had occurred with God, etc.

These hands are now once again assisting this whole process of developing the Revelations and inspired messages received from God two years ago into much greater depth in this next book in the series. Head, heart and hands are working for God.

(*Where's God? Revelations Today*, Bryan Foster, 2018, Great Developments Publishers, Gold Coast, p159-160)

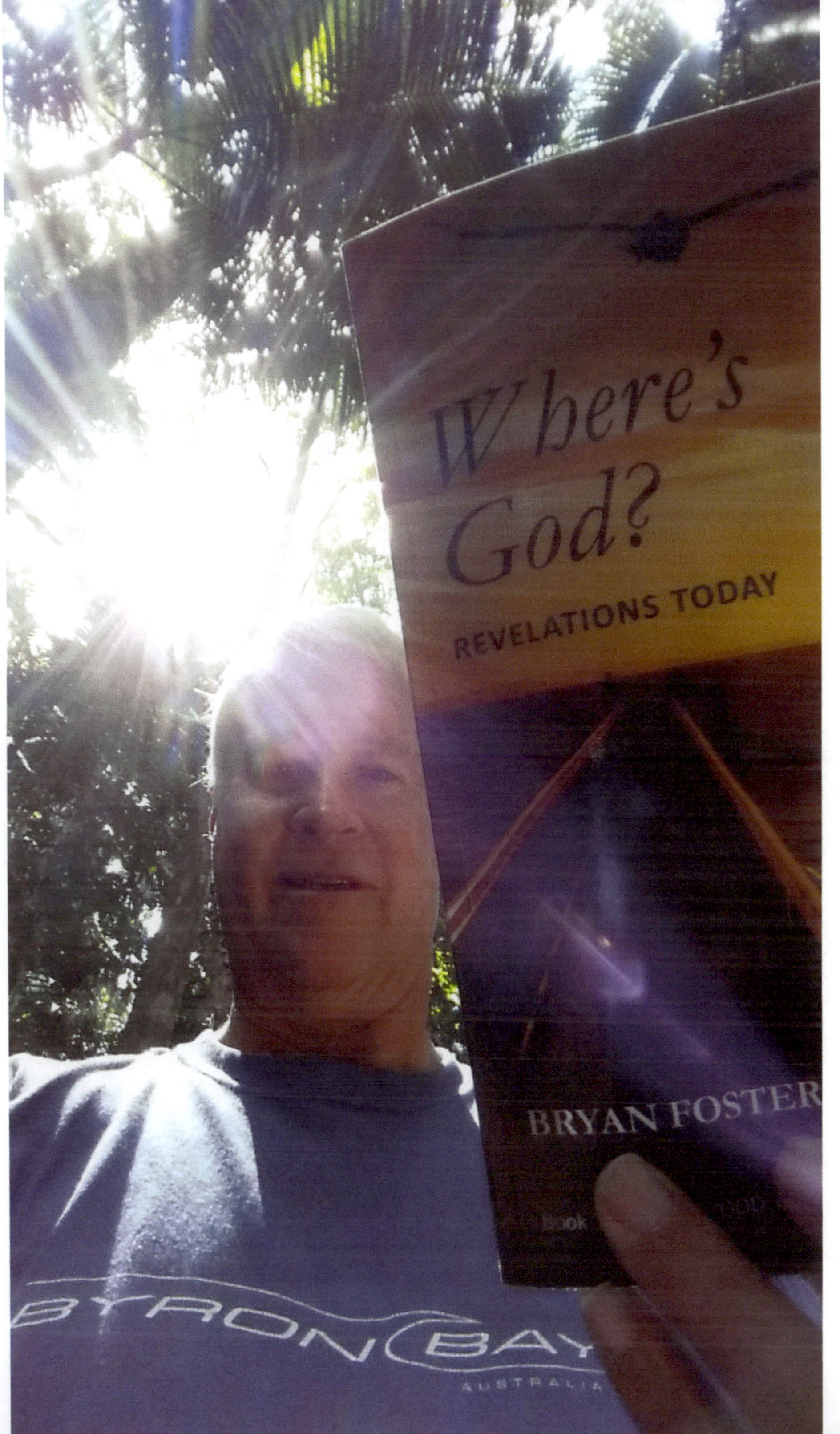

Where's God?
REVELATIONS TODAY
BRYAN FOSTER

1God.world
One God for All
A Discovery of God and God's Messages for Today's World
BRYAN FOSTER
Where's God?
REVELATIONS TODAY
BRYAN FOSTER
Book Three of the 'GOD Today' Series

Coincidence and God's Messages

Have you noticed the coincidences when God was sending you Revelations or inspired messages?

The first significant one in my experiences and recollection comes from the 25th birthday story. God appeared to me through both the Tears from God plus a most revealing heat flowing throughout my body from head to foot while being prayed over. The coincidences include: it was my 25th birthday; it was the last day at this school before leaving to become a principal in a country school; it was the secondary school's Commitment Day to God which I attended for the first time, and I received God most uniquely on this day. Let's now explore some of these coincidences to do with God and the sun as an integral aspect of the above stories.

On Stradbroke Island in May this year when the arrows were received the following coincidences occurred. It was the second anniversary since God gave the afternoon inspired messages on the plains of Mt Warning during the afternoon. These arrows were very similar to ones received earlier this year at the foot of Mt Warning as the sun's arrows were formed when the rays travelled through a tree canopy. On both occasions, I was staying in my caravan/trailer. And the arrows weren't visible until uploaded to a laptop. Combine these with double rainbows to complete the coincidences. These rainbows also happened on the second anniversary, on the same day as the Stradbroke Island sun arrows but in the late afternoon. It was while I was in the same caravan/trailer as where I was revealed to by God. The van was surrounded or pointed to by the double rainbow depending on the viewing angle. From one angle it took on the appearance of the 'pot of gold at the end of a rainbow'.

The cloud sitting atop of Mt Warning image taken the previous year had different coincidences associated. The relatively small puffy cloud was perfectly placed above the peak of the mountain - in various scriptural sources, God comes to the mountain or the people in a cloud. The cloud this day had sunrays emanating outwards in all directions, following the metaphorical theme of God being the sun.

The Easter cross that appeared outside Texas coincidentally appeared the week after Easter. It changed shape from a circular glow to a full dramatic cross as the images progressed. It was 'grounded' in the earth, as the original Jesus' cross would have been. Glowing spectacularly as if the Risen Christ had resurrected the previous Easter Sunday. Not until later in the afternoon did we realised it was the first anniversary of the last time we saw my wife's sister-in-law, Julie, before her unexpected death at fifty. Julie's memorial service concluded with a spectacular sun cross being formed on the room's translucent curtain at sunset – for us it was Julie's cross.

The sun arrow experiences coincidentally occurred at the places my wife and I spent the first years of our lives. Karen was born near Mt Warning, and I lived my first two years on Stradbroke Island.

(*Where's God? Revelations Today*, Bryan Foster, 2018, Great Developments Publishers, Gold Coast, p161-162)

The Magnificent Glorious Sun – Sunrises and Sunsets

The sun figures predominantly in many photos I use from book covers and photobooks to article support images to videos, etc. - and always has. Why? Primarily due to its perceived close association with God through its awesome power and energy which sustain our earthly life. It is the physically closest, spectacular cosmic creation in intensity to God. As the source for maintaining all life on Earth, it holds a central aspect of all our lives. No sun, no life!

Conversely, the sun itself is one continuous multinuclear explosion until it ceases to be. This source of light and energy feeds our earthly life forms. How central and special to our lives.

Who isn't moved by spectacular sunrises and sunsets? Who doesn't enjoy the warmth of the sun during cold periods? And even the opportunity to sunbathe in summer when young or not so (even though known to be dangerous to our health)? To swim, ski, run, ride, walk or paddle in the great outdoors beneath an energising sun? Plus, the sun in all its glory takes the most magnificent photographic and videographic images and video throughout the daylight hours; particularly during the early morning and late afternoon.

The first image was taken from the beach in Far North Queensland at Cape Tribulation in the famous Daintree National Park. It was a beautiful sunrise on my wife's birthday, and the clouds had made a most spectacular shape enclosing the sun but allowing its rays to shoot upwards and downwards out of the clouds. As the sunrise progressed, the clouds opened more and more, each time revealing a more glorious sun with rays growing larger and more intense outwards.

It is the full book cover of the first book in this series: *1God.world: One God for All.* It was a perfect image to highlight the main Revelation of the book, i.e. that there is only One God for the whole world. No one religion. No one name for God. One God who loves all people equally no matter their religion, culture, nationality, colour, wealth, qualifications, interests, etc. It almost appeared that this one almighty God was breaking on through the cover of the cloud to be revealed to all humankind. So in a metaphorical sense, God did break on through to this world and is waiting for us all to break out of this world's clutches and return home to our one, true, creator God.

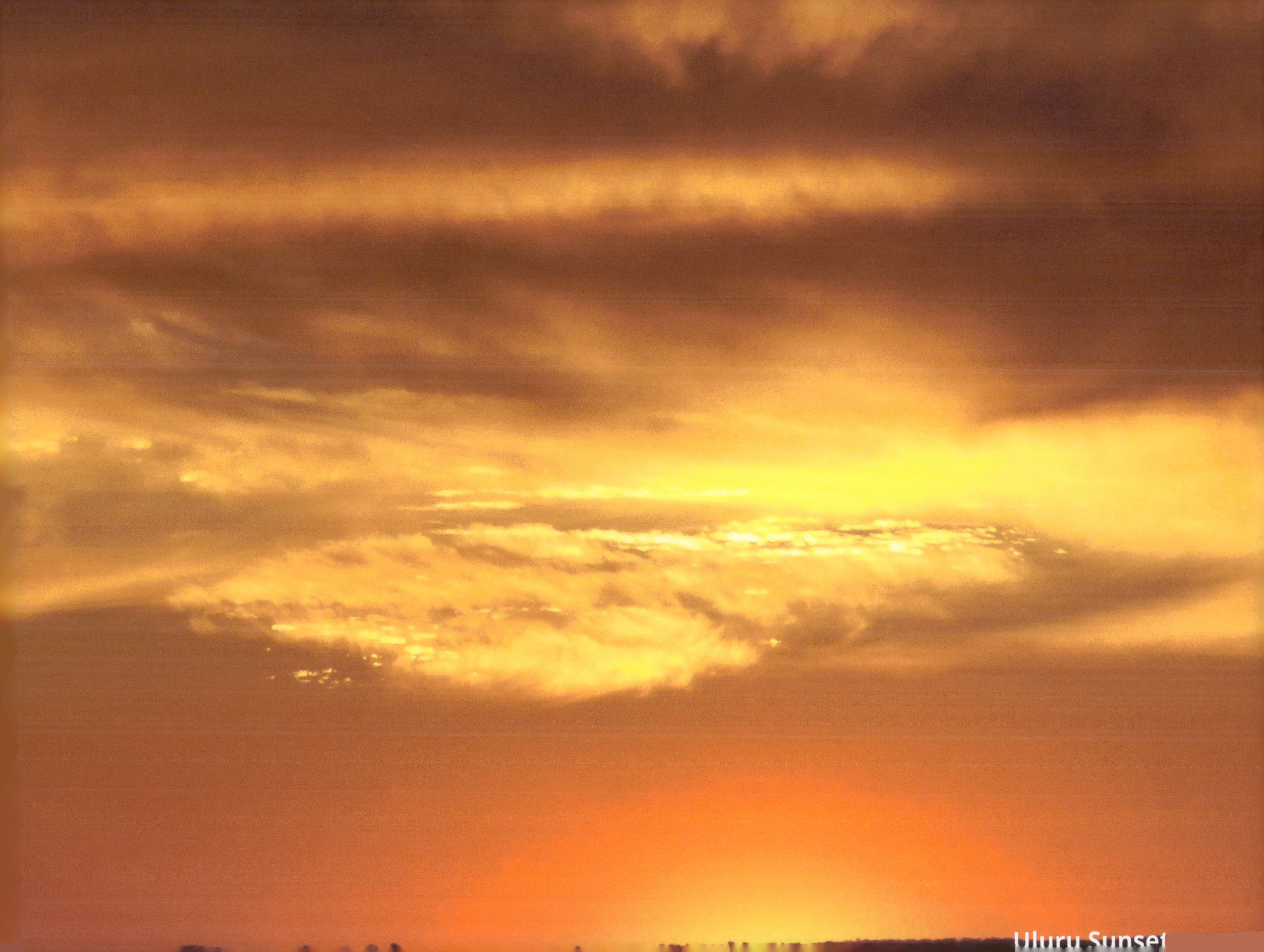
Uluru Sunset

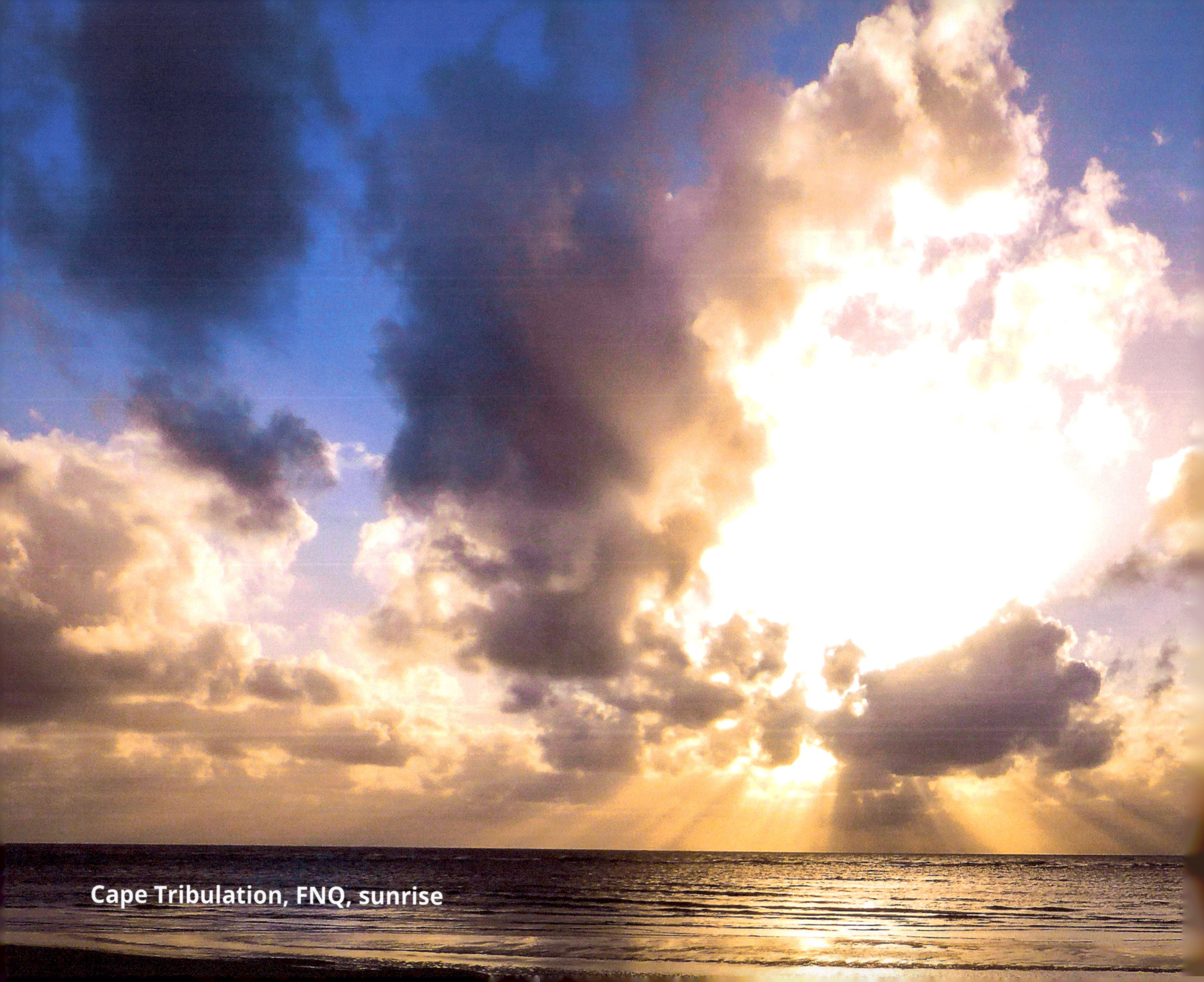
Cape Tribulation, FNQ, sunrise

The second occasion occurred north of the far Western Australian capital of Perth. In tragic circumstances, my sister-in-law by marriage died unexpectantly at the age of fifty. Her memorial service was conducted in an oceanside surf life-saving clubhouse. The ceremony was planned to conclude at exact sunset, so that 'Julie's' sun would set over the ocean witnessed by all those who were present. The beachside window was draped in translucent, cotton fabric, allowing sunlight to penetrate throughout the service. A most remarkable image appeared on the cloth at that sunsetting moment. A single, cross-shaped, sun-created image lit up the cloth and shouted for all to see. Julie was not just setting over her most loved beach, but she was shouting her final farewells through the sun's glorious magnificence.

(*Where's God? Revelations Today*, Bryan Foster, 2018, Great Developments Publishers, Gold Coast, p148-150)

Mullaloo, near Perth

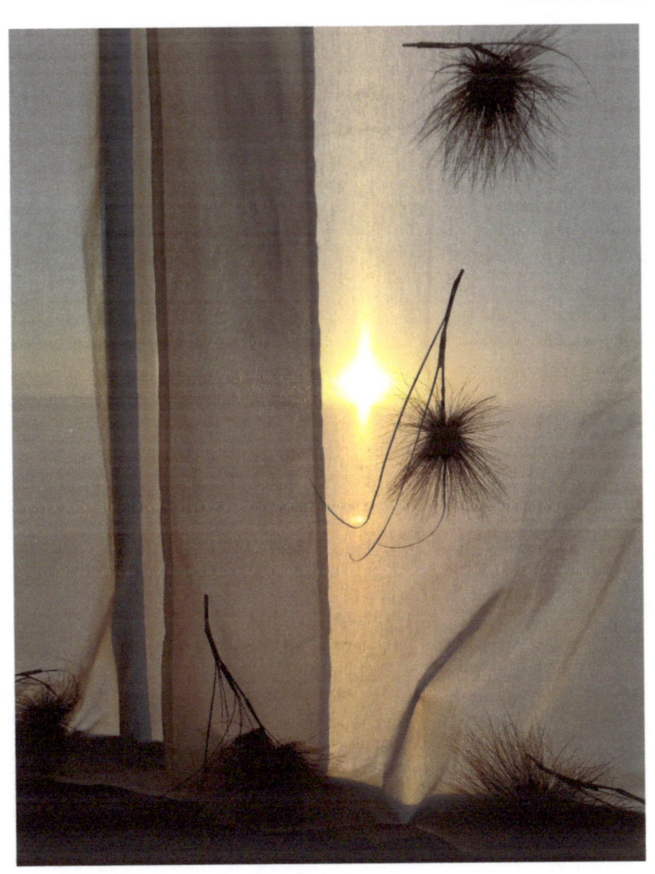

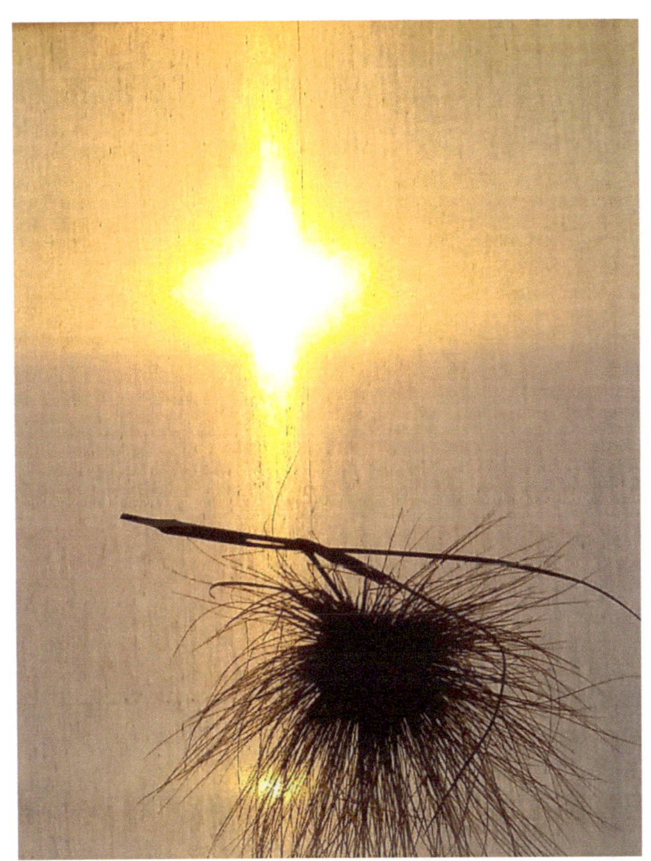

Canada

Vancouver and Vernon, BC

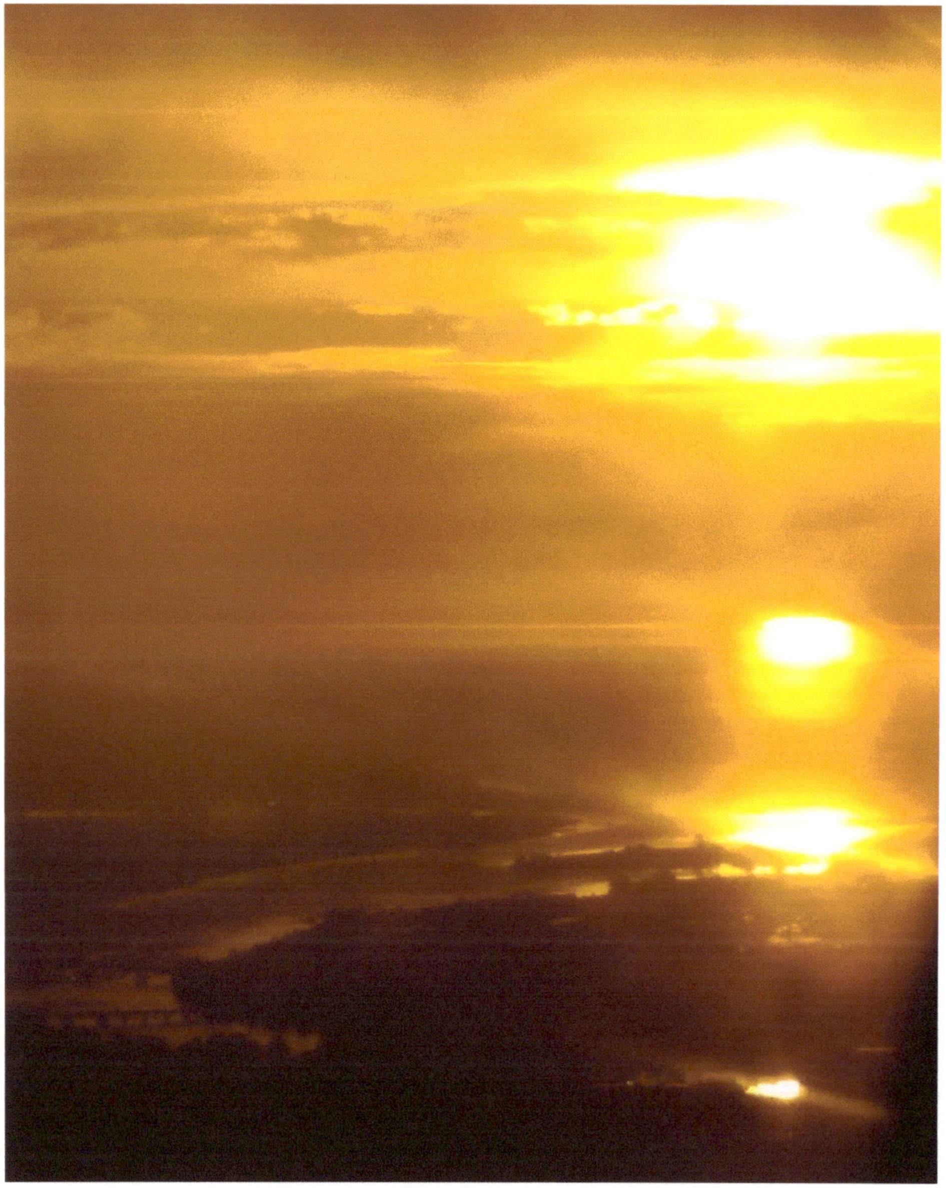

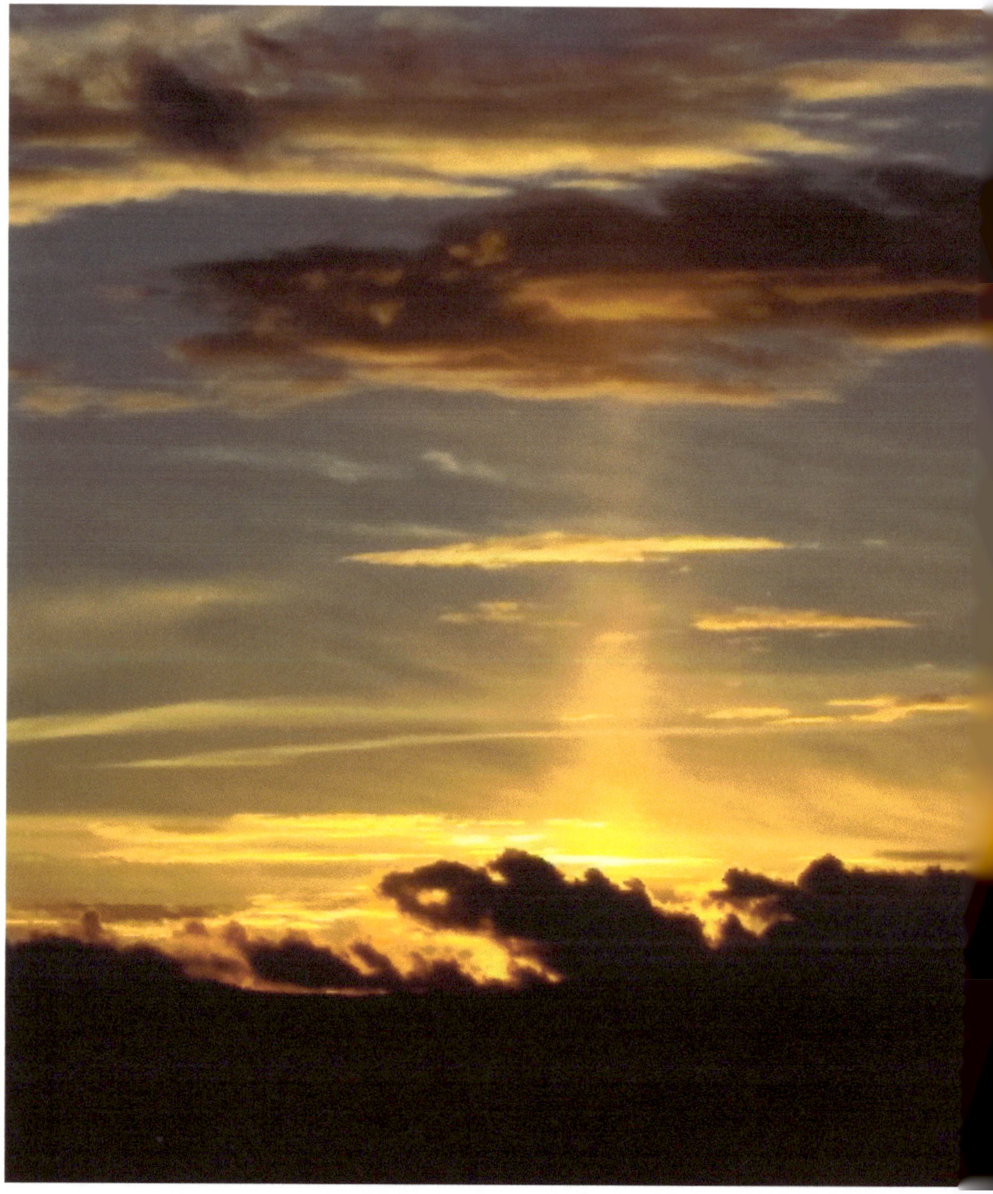

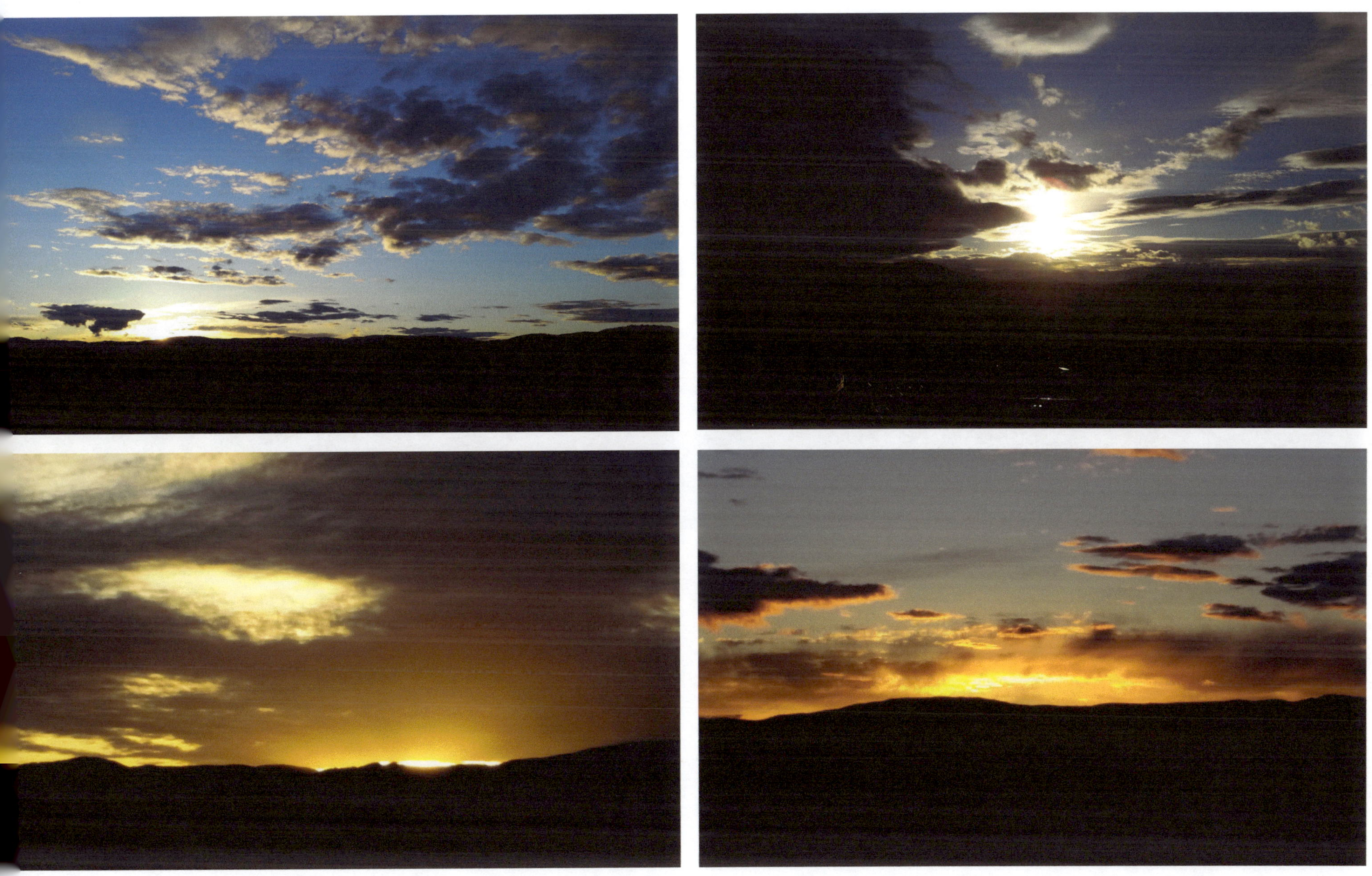

Vernon, BC

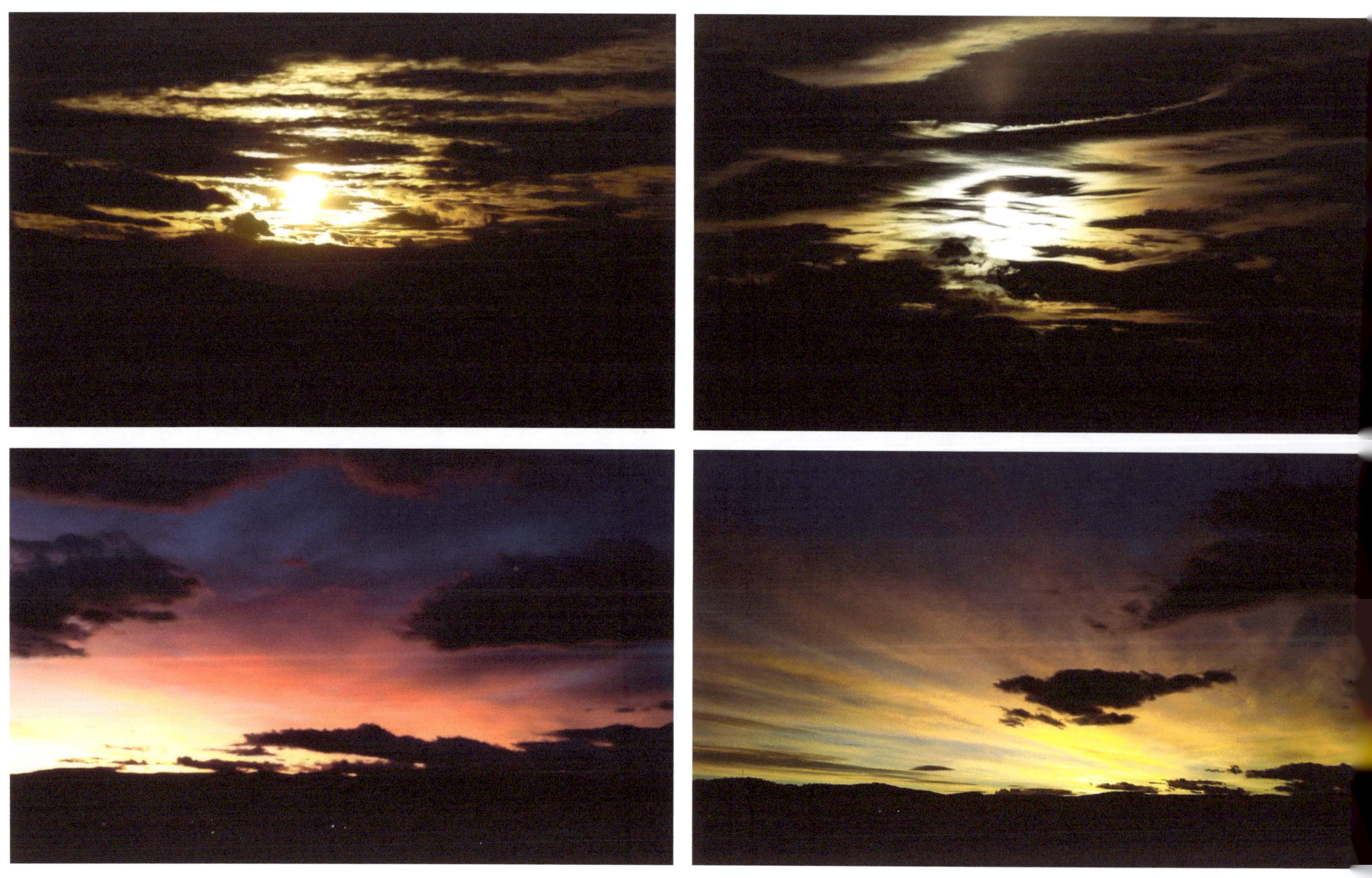

Australia

Amity Point, Stradbroke Island - sunset + Byron Bay – sunrise

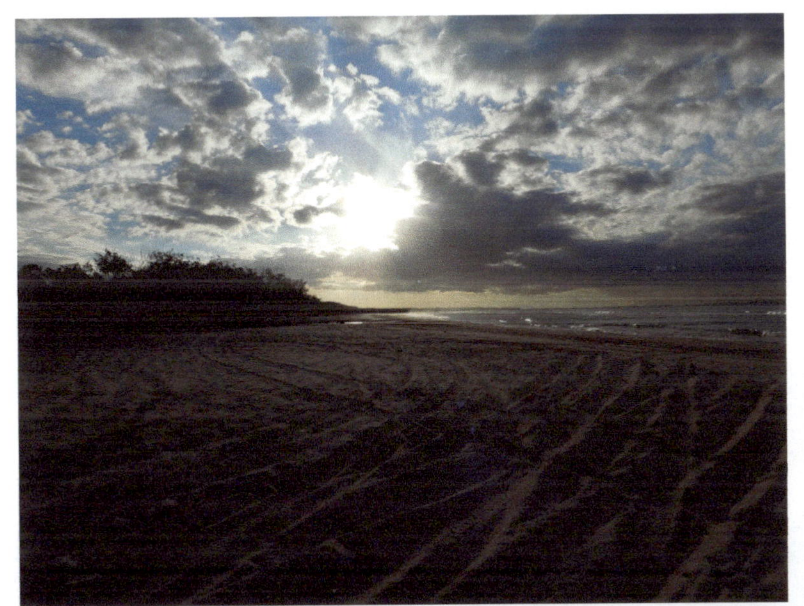

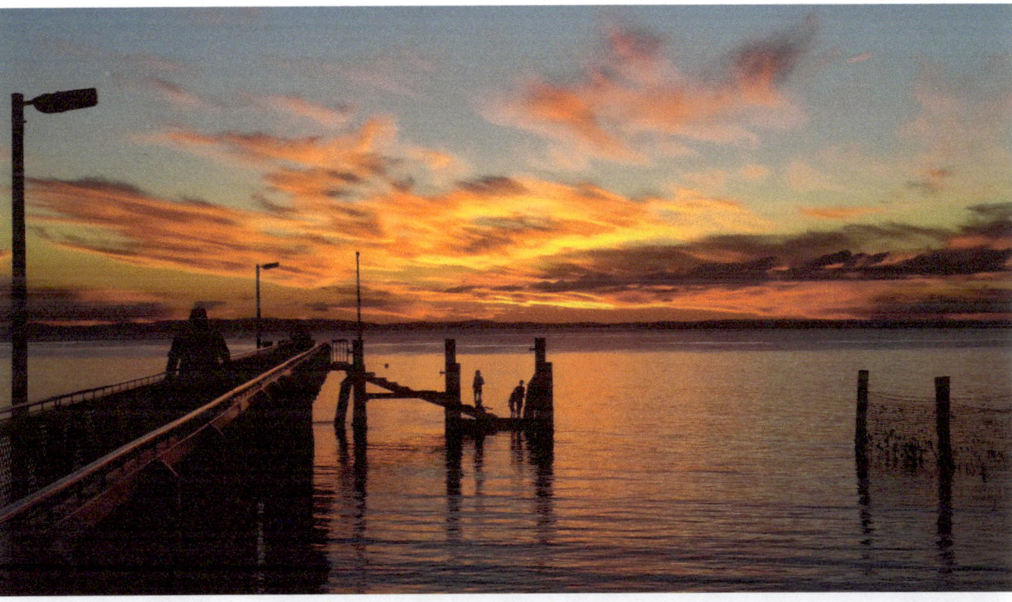

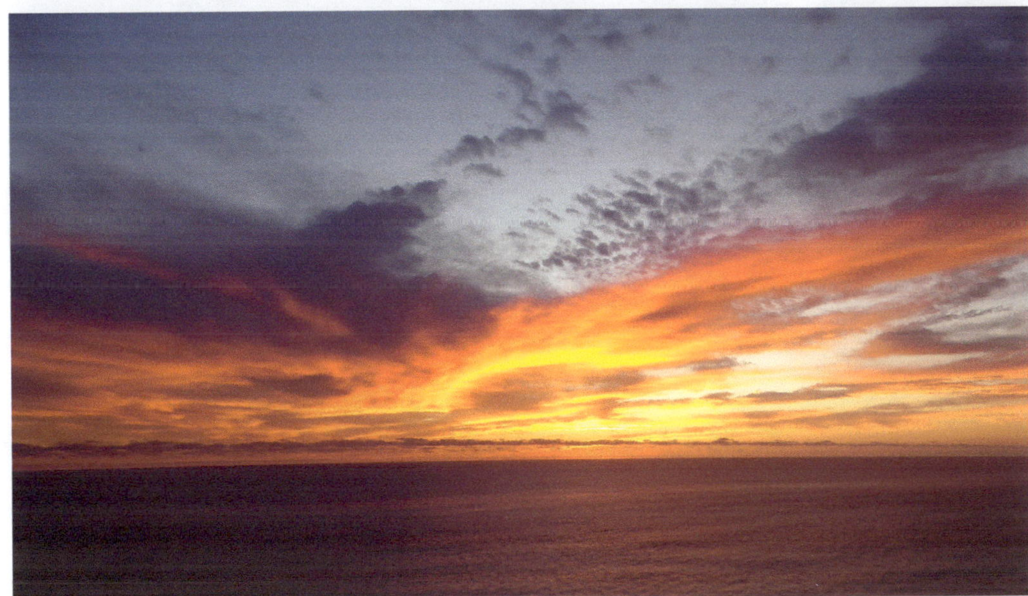

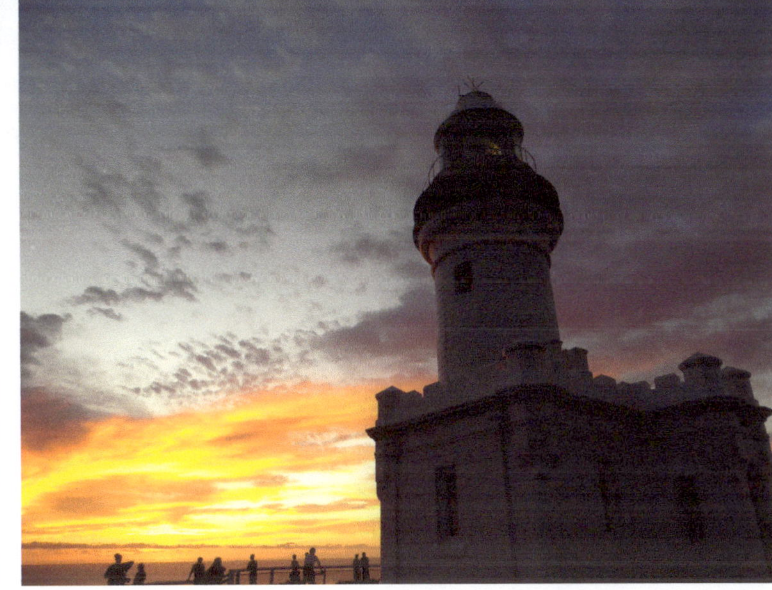

Noosa River, Gold Coast, Murwillumbah and Uluru sunsets

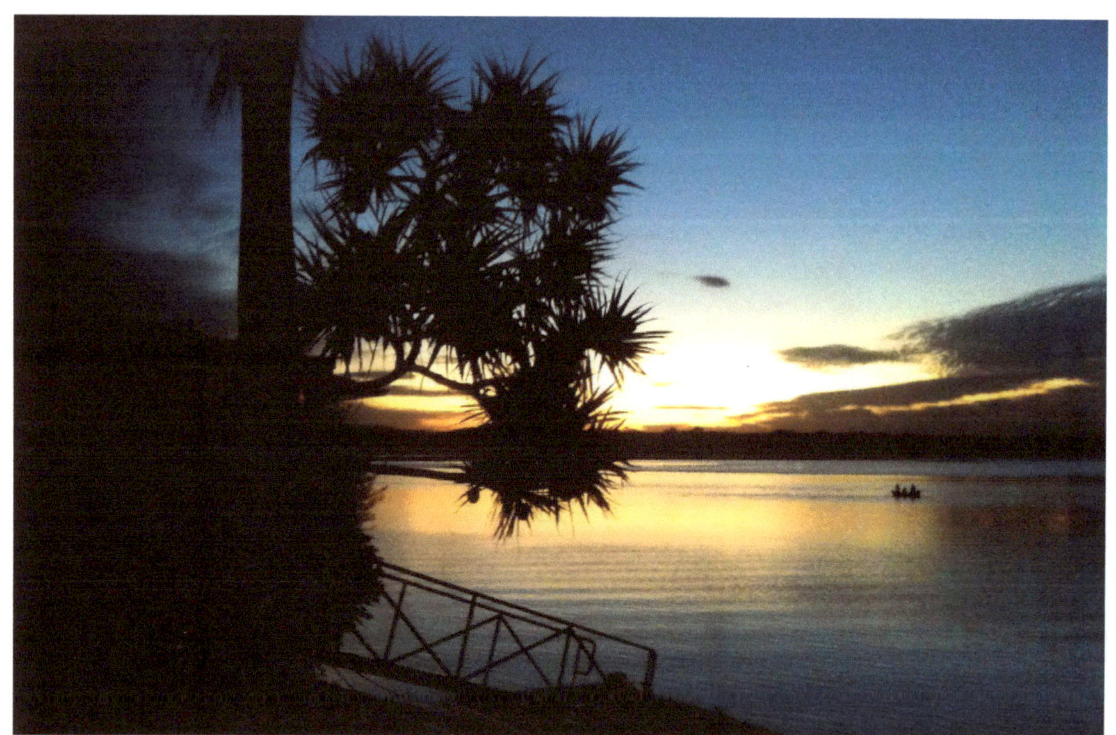

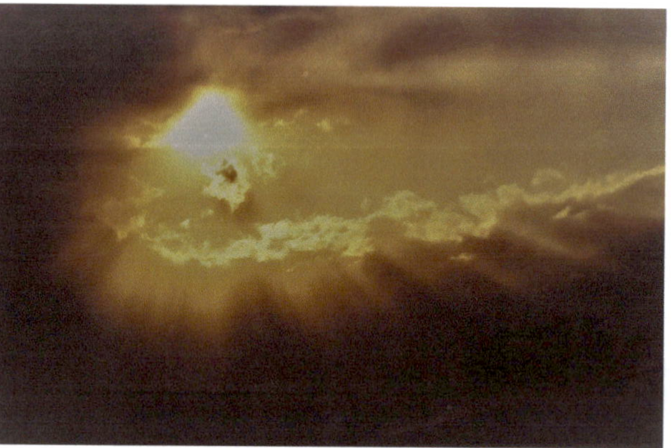

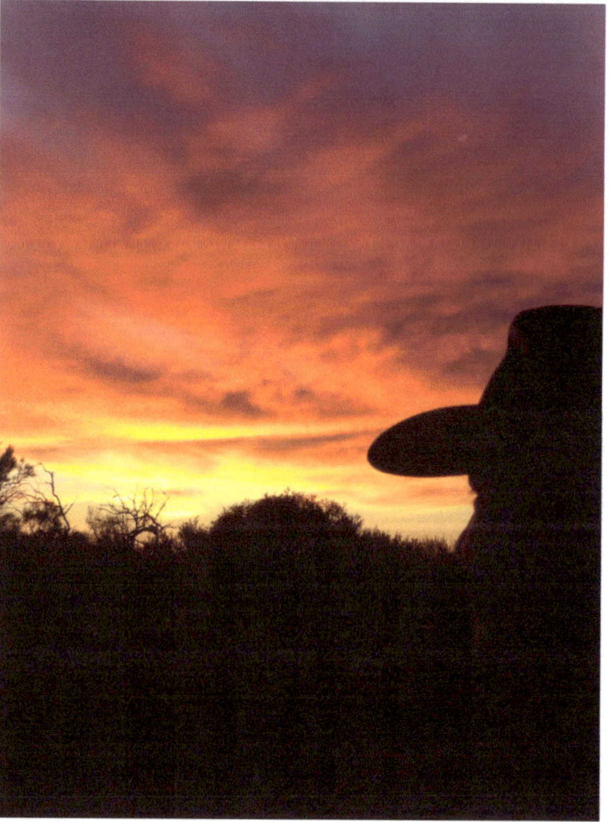

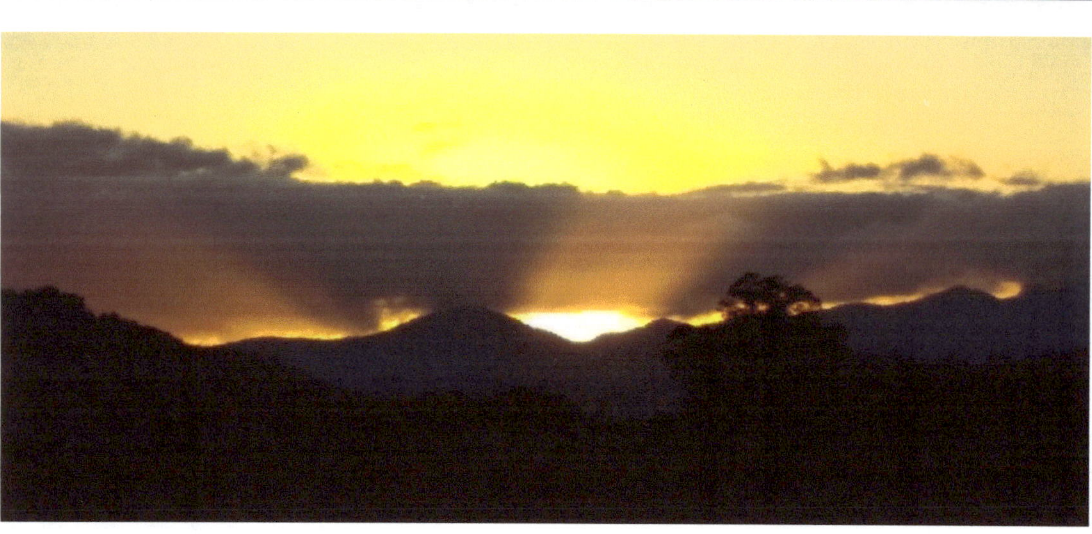

Mt Warning

Revelations and Inspired Messages often occurred around here

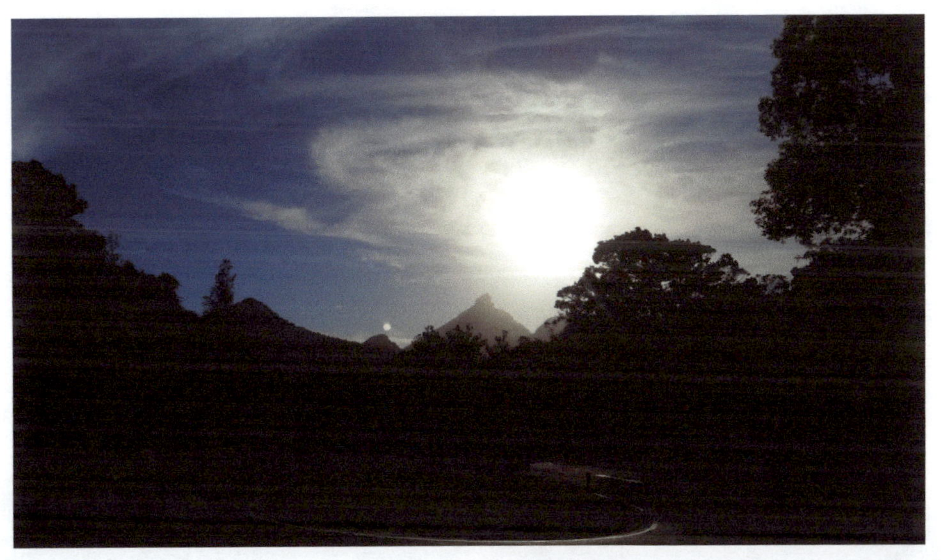

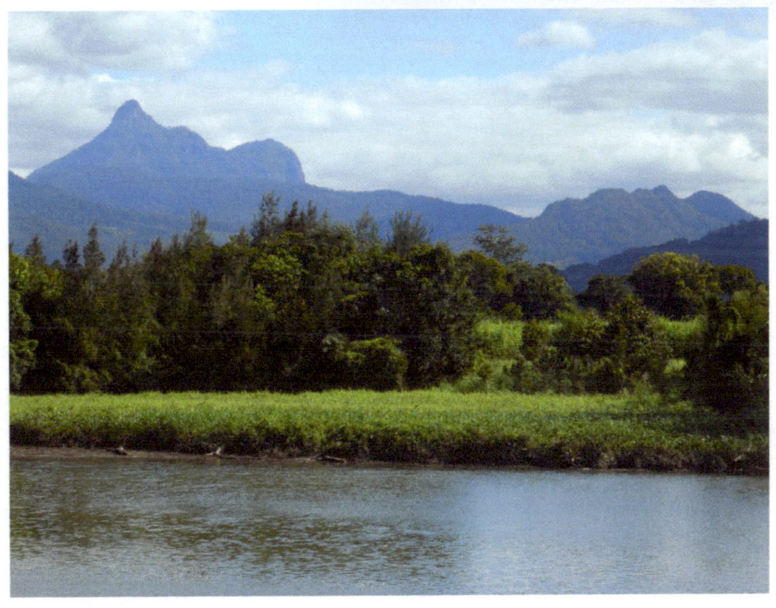

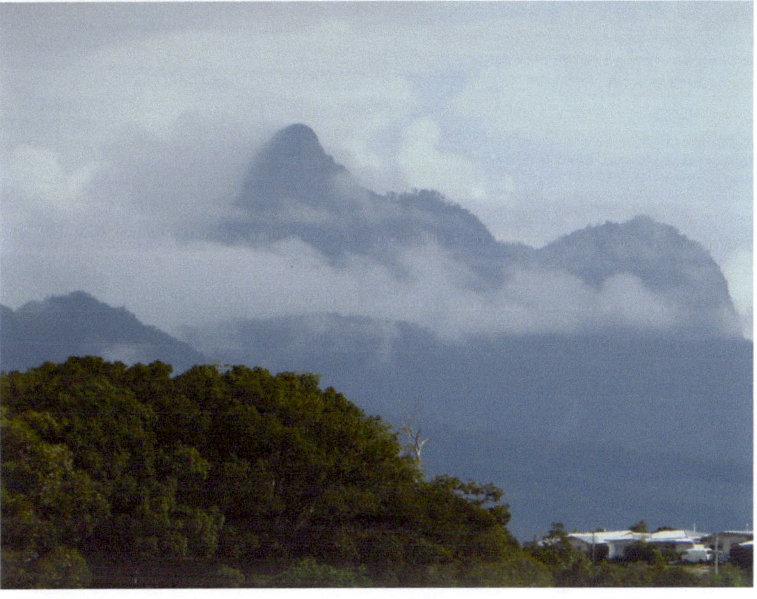

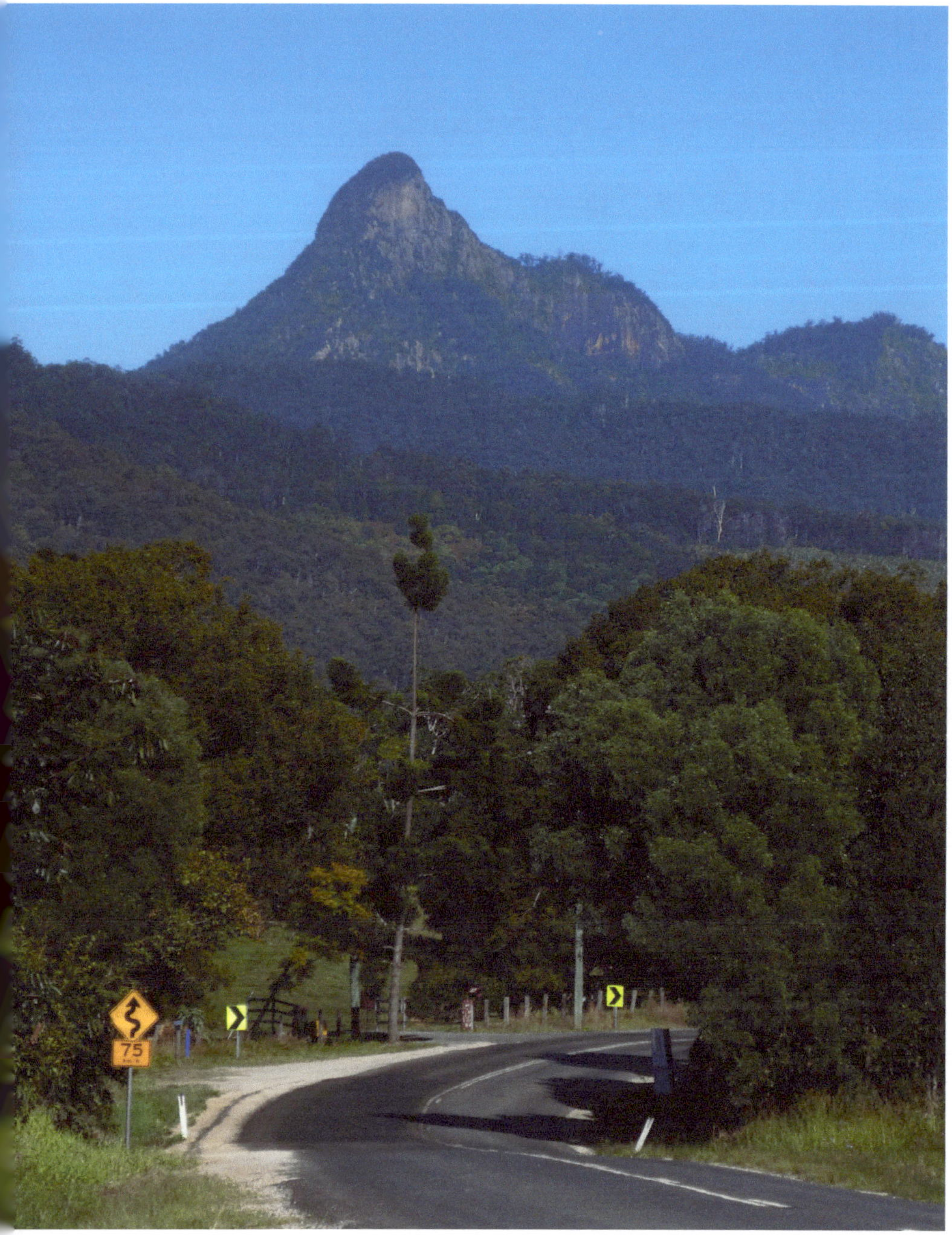

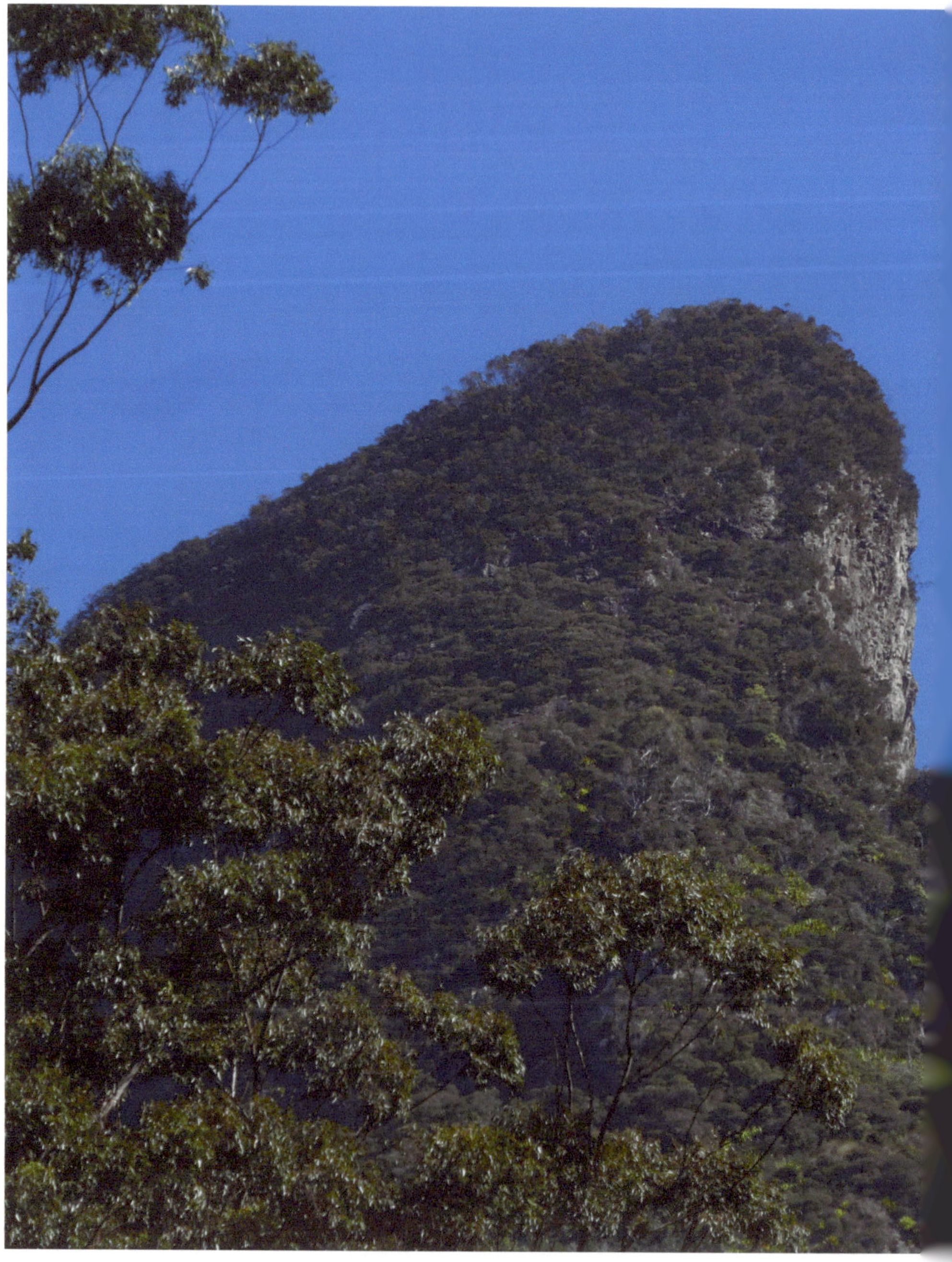

Foot of Mt Warning

Release of *Where's God? Revelations Today*

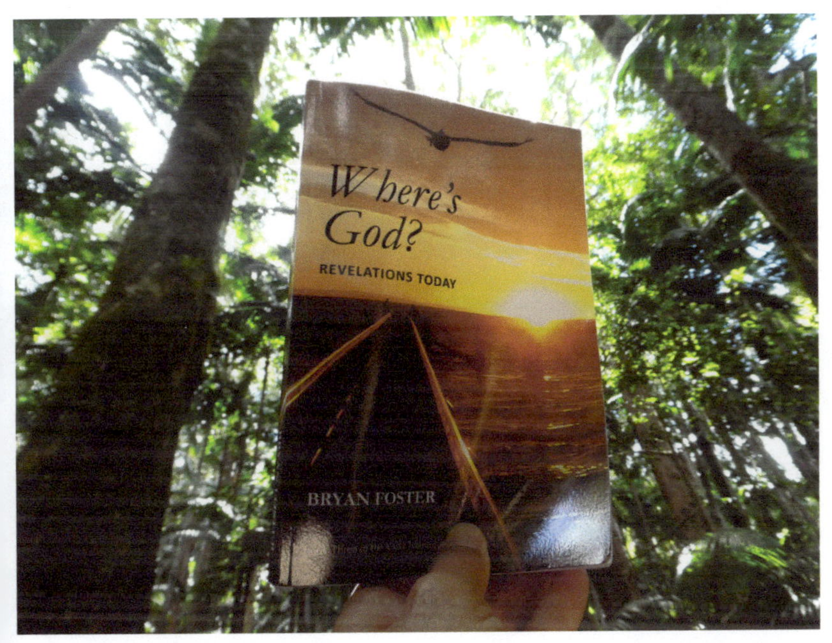
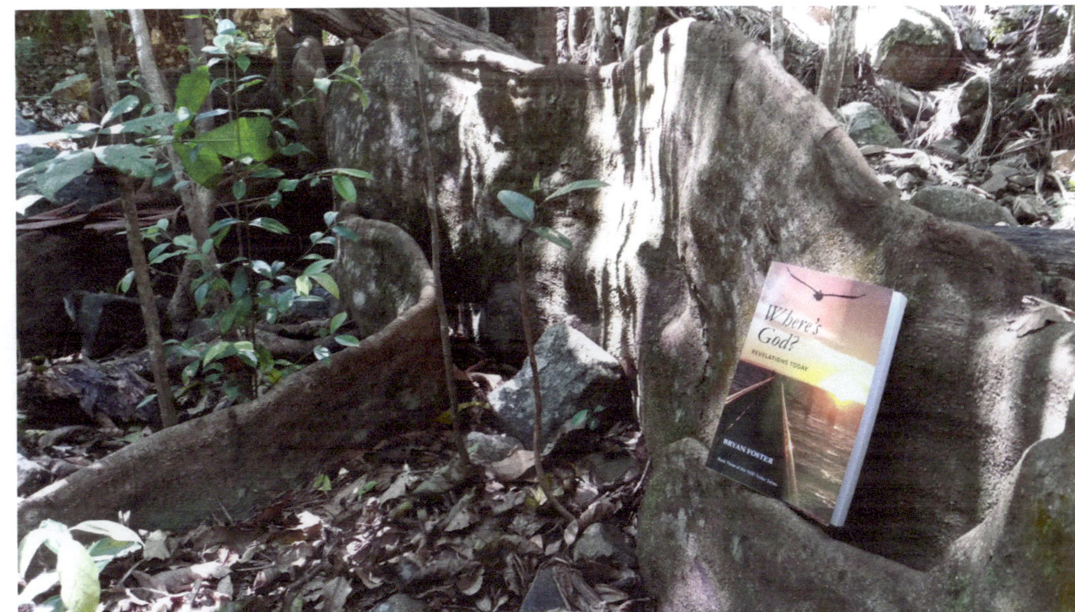

'GOD Today' Series

Book 1: *1God.world: One God for All*, 2016

Book 2: *Mt Warning God's Revelations: Photobook Companion to '1God.world'*, 2017

Book 3: *Where's God? Revelations Today*, 2018

Book 4: *Where's God? Revelations Today: Photobook Companion, (1st and 2nd editions)*, 2018

GOD Today Video Series (2018)

Author's Websites

https://www.godtodayseries.com/- Main website for this series, includes the regularly updated blog commenced in 2016

https://www.bryanfosterauthor.com/ - Author's website

http://www.greatdevelopmentspublishers.com/ - Publisher's website. Original started in 2007

https://www.facebook.com/groups/389602698051426/ - 1God.world Facebook

https://plus.google.com/u/0/ - Google+

https://au.linkedin.com/in/bryanfoster - LinkedIn

https://www.youtube.com/user/efozz1 - 750+ YouTube videos commenced in 2009

https://twitter.com/1Godworld1 - Twitter

https://www.instagram.com/ - Instagram (1godworld)